DAYS TO REMEMBER

DAYS TO REMEMBER

an almanac

by
WILLIAM LIPKIND

illustrated by
JEROME SNYDER

An Astor Book published by Ivan Obolensky, Inc.

© 1961 by William Lipkind and Jerome Snyder

All rights reserved. Published simultaneously in the Dominion of Canada by George J. McLeod Limited, Toronto.

Manufactured in the United States of America

Typography by Accurate Typesetting, Inc.

Designed by Gertrude Goodrich

DAYS TO REMEMBER

Every year is different, and has its own place in history. But every year goes through the same cycle of seasons as the earth moves around the sun. The same days and the same months come again in an orderly procession, over and over, with only a small adjustment, such as Leap Year, needed here and there to keep the count more or less straight.

Long ago men were impressed by the regular movement of the moon, the planets and the stars. They thought that in this harmony of the heavenly bodies lay hidden all the secrets of nature. They thought that what a man is and what happens to him during life receives its direction from the position of the planets at the moment of his birth. Once even scientists believed this; now only the superstitious take any stock in it. Still, we all feel a touch of pleasure when we discover that a famous man whom we admire was born on the same day of the year on which we were born.

In this almanac, for each month of the year you will find the birthdays of a few famous people, and something about them. We have chosen great people in a variety of professions, most of them have not only advanced human culture in a substantial way but are interesting in themselves: religious leaders, statesmen, artists, musicians, writers and scientists. And to represent other fields of achievement that young people are curious about, we have chosen a few men who made their reputation by extraordinary feats: athletes, a dancer, a magician, a tightrope walker. Besides the birthdays you will also find days that are important as holidays, how they came to be celebrated and how they are now celebrated.

To round out the picture of the year, there are bits of natural history about the various seasons, and a few interesting and unusual facts. You can read as you like, either straight through or skipping around. We hope that our brief accounts of people and things will stir you into wanting to know more about them, and lead you to other explorations in the world of books.

JANUARY

*Janus, the god of the door,
had charge of the passage between the past and the future.
The ancient Romans called on him for help
whenever they embarked on a new venture.
They gave his name to the first month of the year,
and pictured him with two faces,
one looking backward at the old year
and the other looking forward to the new year.*

JANUARY

1
New Year's Day

Many people celebrate the new year by getting together with old friends. No matter how bleak the weather is, with friends gathered together and good things on the table the year is well begun. Some take the day as an occasion to make good resolutions. Improvement does not come with a sudden decision but step by step. Nobody ever climbed a mountain with one leap.

Those who make new year's resolutions should remember:
Quickly spoken, quickly broken,
Slow and sure, will endure.

6
Epiphany
or
Twelfth-day

This day is called 'Epiphany,' which means 'showing forth' in Greek, because it is the day Jesus showed himself to the Magi. And it is called 'Twelfth-day' because it is the twelfth day after Christmas. Christmas trees and wreaths are taken down, and the holiday season is ended.

JANUARY

12
BIRTHDAY OF
Charles Perrault ₁₇₂₈

For hundreds of years people told fairy tales but nobody wrote them down. The French writer Perrault was one of the first to put them in a book. He picked such good stories and he told them so well that his tales have become favorites everywhere, among them 'Cinderella,' 'Puss in Boots' and 'Little Red Riding Hood.'

17
BIRTHDAY OF
Benjamin Franklin 1706

Franklin started life with none of the advantages that can smooth the way to a great career. He was one of many children in a family without much money. He had only two years of school. At the age of ten he went to work in his father's business of tallow-chandler and soap-boiler. At thirteen his father apprenticed him to his half-brother James who was in the printing business. Franklin had a vigorous mind and body, and a great store of curiosity, energy and common sense. He educated himself by constant reading of good books, interest in public affairs and observation of nature. At twenty-seven he began to study French, Spanish, Italian and Latin. All his long life, no matter how busy he was, he kept up his studies and found time for work on research and scientific problems.

And what a busy life it was! For many years he was a commercial printer and published a newspaper, 'The Pennsylvania Gazette.' For twenty-five years he wrote and printed 'Poor Richard's Almanack,' the most popular publication of its time. He started the first police force and fire department in the colonies. He took the lead in organizing the militia, in paving the streets, improving street lighting and founding a city hospital. He helped found the University of Pennsylvania and the American Philosophical Society. He served as postmaster and improved the efficiency of the postal service.

Most important of all were his services in the American Revolution. Although a leader of the colonists in the struggle for their rights, he did everything in his power as commissioner in England to arrive at a peaceful settlement. When war broke out he did much to bring about the final victory by his work as ambassador to France. He is the greatest of all American diplomats.

As a scientist and inventor he achieved world fame, although he never had the chance to give his full time to science. His most important contributions were to the study of heat, electricity, weather and navigation. His most important inventions were the lightning rod and the Franklin stove. His most famous experiment is the kite experiment by which he proved that thunder and lightning are due to electricity.

His best book is the story of his life.

JANUARY

19
BIRTHDAY OF
Robert E. Lee 1807

This day is celebrated as a holiday by many southern states. Lee was the outstanding general of the Confederate forces in the Civil War. The way he acted as the losing commander won the admiration and respect of all, both north and south.

20
St. Agnes' Eve

The old belief was that, on this night a girl could see her future husband at the stroke of midnight. Keats wrote a story in verse based on this theme. This is how it begins:

St. Agnes' Eve—Ah, bitter chill it was!
The owl for all his feathers, was a-cold;
The hare limp'd trembling through the frozen grass
And silent was the flock in wooly fold.

On this date the sun enters the sign of Aquarius, the water bearer of the zodiac and remains in that sign until February 19th.

21
BIRTHDAY OF
Lewis Carroll ₁₈₃₂

His real name was Charles Lutwidge Dodgson and he was a mathematician who taught at Oxford. He won fame as Lewis Carroll, the name he used when he published 'Alice's Adventures in Wonderland' and 'Through the Looking Glass.' If you haven't read them, perhaps this small sample will help you decide whether you want to.

> *He thought he saw a Banker's Clerk*
> *Descending from the bus:*
> *He looked again and found it was*
> *A Hippopotamus:*
> *'If this should stay to dine,' he said,*
> *'There won't be much for us.'*

25
BIRTHDAY OF
Robert Burns ₁₇₅₉

He was the great song writer of Scotland. He put words together that went so smoothly with old tunes that they are still sung. His song about old friends, 'Auld Lang Syne,' is a favorite at parties, with everybody joining in the chorus.

27
BIRTHDAY OF
Wolfgang
Amadeus Mozart ₁₇₅₆

Mozart was a boy who was born for music. His father, Leopold Mozart, was a good musician, and Wolfgang was brought up in a house full of music. He learned it faster than it was taught to him. At three years of age he had begun to play the harpsichord. By the time he was six he could play well on the violin and organ. The most wonderful thing was that from the start he not only played the music that he heard but easily made up music of his own.

He began playing in public at five and his father took him all over Germany when he was six. The next year they went to France and the year after that to England. Everywhere Mozart played at court for kings, queens, and the nobility.

Everywhere people were amazed at the little boy's genius. The most famous musicians of the time came to listen to him and joined the others in praising and admiring him. In spite of all these honors, the boy Mozart remained simple and natural. He did not become proud. He had the greatest respect for his father and tried to please him in every way.

When Mozart was thirteen his father took him to Italy. Italy at that time was the home of music where all the best musicians lived. There he was given every honor. He played in all the big cities. By this time Mozart was writing one piece of music after another; music of every kind for all the instruments and for voice.

What a pity it is that Mozart with so much to give to the world had such a short life! He died at thirty-five, writing music to the end. His last years were not as happy as his youth. He became poor and could not get the help he needed. But nothing could stop the flow of his music. In his short life he wrote more than six hundred compositions. His operas, "Don Giovanni," "The Marriage of Figaro" and "The Magic Flute" are among the greatest ever written. His symphonies, his concertos, his quartets, have never been surpassed. Much of what he wrote is great and all of it is good.

A SONG FOR JANUARY MORNINGS

It's nice to get up in the morning when the sun begins to shine,
At four or five or six o'clock in the good old summertime;
But when the snow is snowing, and it's murky overhead—
It's nice to get up in the morning—but it's nicer to lie in bed.

SIR HARRY LAUDER

JANUARY

THE CATERPILLAR PARADE

The great French naturalist Henri Fabre spent his whole life studying insects. Once he decided to make an experiment with processional caterpillars. These are caterpillars that march, one behind the other, following a leader and spinning a thread as they go.

Fabre managed to get the line of caterpillars marching around a large vase. The parade made a complete circle around the vase, caterpillar after caterpillar, with no leader at all. It was at midday on a January thirtieth that Fabre got them started. When night came the caterpillars were still marching.

The next morning they were still going. The next day they were still going. Although they were numb from the cold and weak from lack of food they did not stop. They could not break away from their fixed habit of following the leader. And they could not even figure out that in this case they did not have a real leader. At last, after eighty-four hours of continual marching, the line broke, purely by accident.

The tiny caterpillars had marched more than a quarter of a mile without stop, going around the vase. This is an example of behavior based on instinct without any use of reason.

JEREMY CRABAPPLE says:

*It's asking too much of an alarm clock
to expect it to stir a sleepy boy out of a cozy bed
on a frosty morning.*

FEBRUARY

*The shortest month of the year,
and yet so long if you are tired of winter.
The new school term has begun,
and spring is just around the corner.
The ancient Romans also gave this month its name.
They had ceremonies at this time to make themselves pure.
And so they called the month 'February'
from the Latin word 'februare' which means 'to make pure.'*

FEBRUARY

2
Ground-Hog Day

According to an old legend, the ground-hog, or woodchuck, comes out of his burrow on this day. If he sees his shadow, there will be six more weeks of winter, and he goes back to sleep. If he does not see his shadow, he stays up because winter is nearly over.

7

BIRTHDAY OF

Charles Dickens 1812

Dickens was a bright boy, quick to learn and something of a show-off. His mother taught him to read, and he read everything he could lay his hands on. At the age of seven he was sent to school. Two years later bad luck struck his family. His father was put in jail because he couldn't pay money he owed, and Charles was set to work in a factory. All day long he had to tie up and label pots of blacking to earn his living. He had little to eat and slept in a cold attic.

When Charles was twelve his father inherited some money and sent him to boarding school for two years. He then went to work as errand boy for a lawyer. He never forgot his misery in the factory, and spent every free moment in study. At sixteen he began as a reporter. Three years later he had reached the top of the profession and by the time he was twenty-one he was writing original articles for magazines.

His fame began with his book, 'Pickwick Papers.' Everybody read it and talked about it. The many funny characters and incidents in the story made people laugh. And they laughed all the more because they felt there was something serious about it too. Dickens understood all that was sad in life. His own troubles made him able to feel what others suffered. He became the champion of the poor and the weak and he attacked the laws of his time which favored the rich and were harsh to the poor.

FEBRUARY

Dickens wrote many books, and all of them are good. Perhaps the best are those based on his own childhood. 'David Copperfield' and 'Great Expectations' are the two novels which show must fully his sympathy for young people and the problems they have to face in finding their way in the world.

11
BIRTHDAY OF
Thomas Alva Edison 1847

Edison is best known for his invention of the phonograph and the motion-picture, but during his long life he made many other inventions, most of them in the field of electricity. His scientific interest began early. At the age of 12, while working as a newsboy on a train, he made experiments in chemistry. At fifteen he became a telegraph operator. So absorbed was he in his studies and his experiments in electricity that he sometimes forgot to attend to his job. Even when he had become rich and famous, he spent his days, and often his nights, in the laboratory, hardly stopping to sleep when his mind was on a problem.

At his death he held hundreds of patents, many of them very important in modern life.

FEBRUARY

12
BIRTHDAY OF
Abraham Lincoln ₁₈₀₉

The year before Lincoln was elected President, in a speech in Cincinnati, he made this statement:

> *I hold, if the Almighty had ever made a set of men that should do all the eating and none of the work, He would have made them with mouths only and no hands; and if He had ever made another class that He intended should do all the work and none of the eating, He would have made them without mouths and with all hands.*

FEBRUARY

14
Saint Valentine's Day

This is the time for valentines. It's best to write your own, but if you can't, here's one that will do for anybody:

If you were only mine
I'd be as true as true
I'd have no other valentine
But you and only you.

19
Pisces

The sign of Pisces, the Fish, begins on this day and ends on March 21.

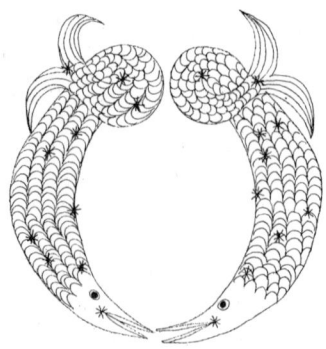

FEBRUARY

22
BIRTHDAY OF
George Washington 1732

Great men are seldom judged at their true value in their own time. The people who know them well see all the little faults, and often miss the greatness. But Washington was respected even by those who knew him best. His political opponent, Thomas Jefferson, wrote a description of him in a letter:

... He was incapable of fear, meeting personal dangers with the calmest unconcern ... His integrity was most pure, his justice the most inflexible I have ever known ... He was indeed in every sense of the words, a wise, a good, and a great man ... His person, you know, was fine, his stature exactly what one would wish, his deportment easy, erect and noble; the best horseman of his age, and the most graceful figure that could be seen on horseback ...

On the whole, his character was, in its mass, perfect, in nothing bad, in few points indifferent; and it may be truly said, that never did nature and fortune combine more perfectly to make a man great ...

FEBRUARY

23
BIRTHDAY OF
George Frederick Handel 1685

One of the greatest musicians of all time, Handel, like Mozart, was a child prodigy, but did not have such an easy start. His father was a barber-surgeon with not much use for music, and he wanted his son to become a lawyer. A friend smuggled a clavichord into the attic of Handel's house. This instrument has a small sound, and with the door closed, the little boy could safely practice. When he was seven years old his father went to visit an older son who was valet to a German duke and took him along. There he made friends with the court musicians and was permitted to practice on the organ. One day when he was playing, the duke heard him, saw his talent and persuaded his father to let him study music. When he was twelve he was sent to Berlin where he played at Court. He made such an impression that the prince offered to send him to Italy to finish his musical education. But his father refused, still hoping to make a lawyer of him, and back home he went.

Later on he became a church organist. When he was twenty his first opera, 'Almira,' was produced in Hamburg with great success. From there he went to Italy where he achieved great fame both as a composer and a performer. Three years later he was offered the position of chief musician to the Elector of Hanover, an important German prince. He accepted on condition that he could first go to England for a while. In England he was so successful as an opera composer and had such a good time that he forgot all about the job in Germany. Imagine how he felt a few years later when the Elector of Hanover came to the throne of England as George I! He won his pardon and got into the king's good graces with his famous Water Music which was performed at a royal water party on the Thames.

He ran his own theater in London and produced many operas. Then he turned from the opera to the oratorio. At this point he wrote the works which are still played and on which his present fame largely rests. The greatest of them is the "Messiah" which is given at Christmas in churches and concert halls everywhere in the world.

The strange thing about Handel is that he began as a German with training in German music, became a great master of Italian opera, and wound up as an Englishman and the most important English composer.

ONE MAN BAND

In the early 1800's Archduke Charles of Austria bought a huge instrument called the panomonico which could be played by one man. It had in it 150 flutes, 150 flageolets, 2 timbals and 3 large drums. Charles was not a music lover; he got it just to annoy people of his court.

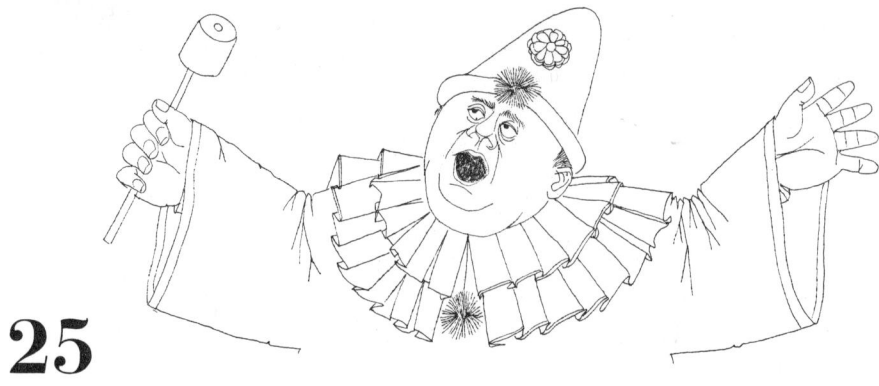

25
BIRTHDAY OF
Enrico Caruso 1873

Caruso was the most famous singer in the world in a time of many great singers. For all his fame and riches he remained the simple boy of Naples who fought his way up from poverty. Caruso was warm-hearted, kind, full of jokes and high spirits. Caruso died in 1929. Luckily we still can listen to records of the singing of this wonderful tenor.

Most people seem to think that skiing is a new winter sport but a Latin historian 1500 years ago wrote about skiing, and it must have been quite old in his time.

28
BIRTHDAY OF
Vaslav Nijinsky 1890

Many people consider Nijinsky the greatest dancer of all time. He had every talent a dancer needs. His training, which began when he was only three, had given him a perfect mastery of the art. He had an extraordinary body. He was a wonderful actor. He was a sensitive musician. And he had a personal vividness that made him seem to shine when he was on the stage. The people who saw him dance always talk of his amazing leaps. He covered the entire stage in one leap and seemed to float in the air.

FEBRUARY

THE SPEED OF BIRDS

Anybody who has ever watched birds streak across the sky must wonder how fast they go. Most small birds have a top speed of 45 to 50 miles an hour. Pigeons can fly as fast as 65. The record speed for wild ducks and geese is 70. The fastest small bird is the swift; he shoots up to 170 miles an hour. The fastest of all birds are hawks. The duck hawk, when going after its prey, comes pretty close to hitting 200 miles an hour.

JEREMY CRABAPPLE says:

*Don't put more into your sack
Than you can carry on your back.*

MARCH

*In olden times the year began in March.
And doesn't it seem more natural to begin the year
with the spring rather than in midwinter as we now do?
The name of this month comes from the Roman god of war, Mars.
Perhaps he was a spring god before he became a war god.
Or perhaps the Romans chose his name for the month
because they thought it a good time for war.*

MARCH

1
St. David's Day

This is a Welsh holiday, as St. David is the patron saint of Wales. Welshmen mark it by wearing a leek on their hats. The leek, the emblem of Wales, is a plant of the lily family like its cousin, the onion.

5
BIRTHDAY OF
Howard Pyle 1853

One of the greatest American illustrators, Pyle was also an excellent writer. All his books have interesting pictures and make good reading. Best of all, because they are most exciting, are his books for boys, 'Robin Hood,' 'Men of Iron' and 'Otto of the Silver Hand.'

Water expands when it freezes. Ice contracts when it melts. That's why ice floats on top of water; it's less dense. And it's also the reason a bottle full of water will break when it freezes. The expanding water cracks the glass.

MARCH

6
BIRTHDAY OF
Michelangelo 1475

His full name was Michelangelo Buonarroti, but he is always called just by his first name. He is one of the greatest artists of all time. His father was a merchant. Soon after his birth, his mother being sickly, he was left in the country in the care of a nurse. She was the wife of a stonecutter, and Michelangelo grew up with the sound of stonework in his ears. He saw the masons set their chisels on the crude stone and hammer away with their mallets.

When he was ten, his father took him to Florence and put him in school. To follow in his father's footsteps and be a merchant he would have to learn how to read and write and keep accounts. The boy, however, did not want to be a merchant. He had one ambition: to be a sculptor. The trouble was that in those times people of his father's class looked down on all artists and especially sculptors. And his father would not consent.

His father held out for three years, then seeing that he could not change the boy's mind, gave in. But since painting was a little more gentlemanly than sculpture, he apprenticed him to the Ghirlandajo brothers who were painters. One of them, Domenico, was the best fresco painter of the time. Fresco is the art of painting on wet plaster so that the colors become part of the wall when the plaster is dry. Now that he was free to follow his bent, the boy threw himself into the work with all his strength. By the time he was fifteen he had mastered the skills of painting and was almost ready to begin on his own. Then another opportunity came his way.

With the consent of his master Domenico he entered the school of sculpture kept by the ruler of Florence, Lorenzo the Magnificent. For the first time he could do what he really wanted, work with stone. He moved forward with the same force in sculpture as he had in painting. At the same time he was able to learn many other things from the brilliant men at the court of Lorenzo, himself a fine poet and a serious student of art and philosophy.

He began his career as a mature artist, working both as painter and sculptor. Later in life, he turned to poetry, writing sonnets with the same depth of feeling. His last years were devoted to architecture. He was in the midst of great projects when he died just before ninety.

His most amazing work is the painting of the Sistine Chapel in Rome. The huge frescoes of the ceiling took almost five years. Most of this time, Michelangelo had to lie on his back on the scaffold. Every stroke of color had to be put on with perfect accuracy, for there is no chance to correct in fresco. And meanwhile drops of paint were dripping on his face from the wet plaster on the ceiling above him.

The fresco wall in the Sistine Chapel, the Last Judgment, is the most famous single painting in the world. His greatest architectural piece is the wonderful dome of St. Peter's in Rome. Among the best of his many great sculptures are the 'Moses' now in Rome and the tombs in the Medici Chapel in Florence.

THE LEMMING

The lemming is a small Scandinavian mouse. Every few years a huge tribe of lemmings will start migrating. They travel by night, and eat and sleep by day. They go downhill, eating up everything they can in the country they pass through. On the way they are followed by beasts of prey of all sorts, who live off them. They cross rivers and lakes, moving straight down through the valleys to the sea. When they reach the sea they plunge in and swim straight out until they drown. Where are the lemmings bound for? Why does nothing stop their march but death? We can only guess. But it's easy to see why people talk of any wild venture as a march of lemmings.

The old belief that snakes suck milk from cows has no basis in fact. The so-called milk snakes that live near barns and stables have no interest in milk. They are there to prey on the rodents who are attracted wherever cattle fodder is stored.

NAMES

You may think that you have a very common name, if your name happens to be John or William, and you're right. But the most common name in the world is Mahomet, which is spelled in a dozen different ways. The shortest name is a Burmese name, written 'H. You can make your own guess how it is pronounced!

MARCH 14

BIRTHDAY OF Albert Einstein 1879

If any man deserves to be singled out as the greatest of all scientists, it is Sir Isaac Newton. If any other man deserves to be placed beside Newton, it is Albert Einstein. Each in his time brought together the work of many scientists before him and invented theories that changed all thought after him. They were both men of powerful mind, wide imagination and mathematical genius. Both were religious, but somewhat differently. Neither showed signs of great ability in early school days. But here the resemblance ends.

Newton was a man of strange character. He was proud, irritable and suspicious. He hid his thoughts from others. Einstein was as great as a man as he was as a scientist. He was kind, modest and open, as gentle as he was firm. His strongest desire was to understand the laws of the universe. And above all he wanted to be of service to mankind.

When the Nazis came to power in Germany, they took away Einstein's citizenship because he was a Jew. Every American should feel proud that the United States then lived up to its great tradition of hospitality. Einstein came to the Institute for Higher Study at Princeton as professor of mathematics, became an American citizen, and spent the rest of his life here.

A SONG FOR MARCH

Who has seen the wind?
Neither I nor you:
But when the leaves hang trembling,
The wind is passing through.
Who has seen the wind?
Neither you nor I:
But when the trees bow down their heads,
The wind is passing by.

CHRISTINA ROSSETTI

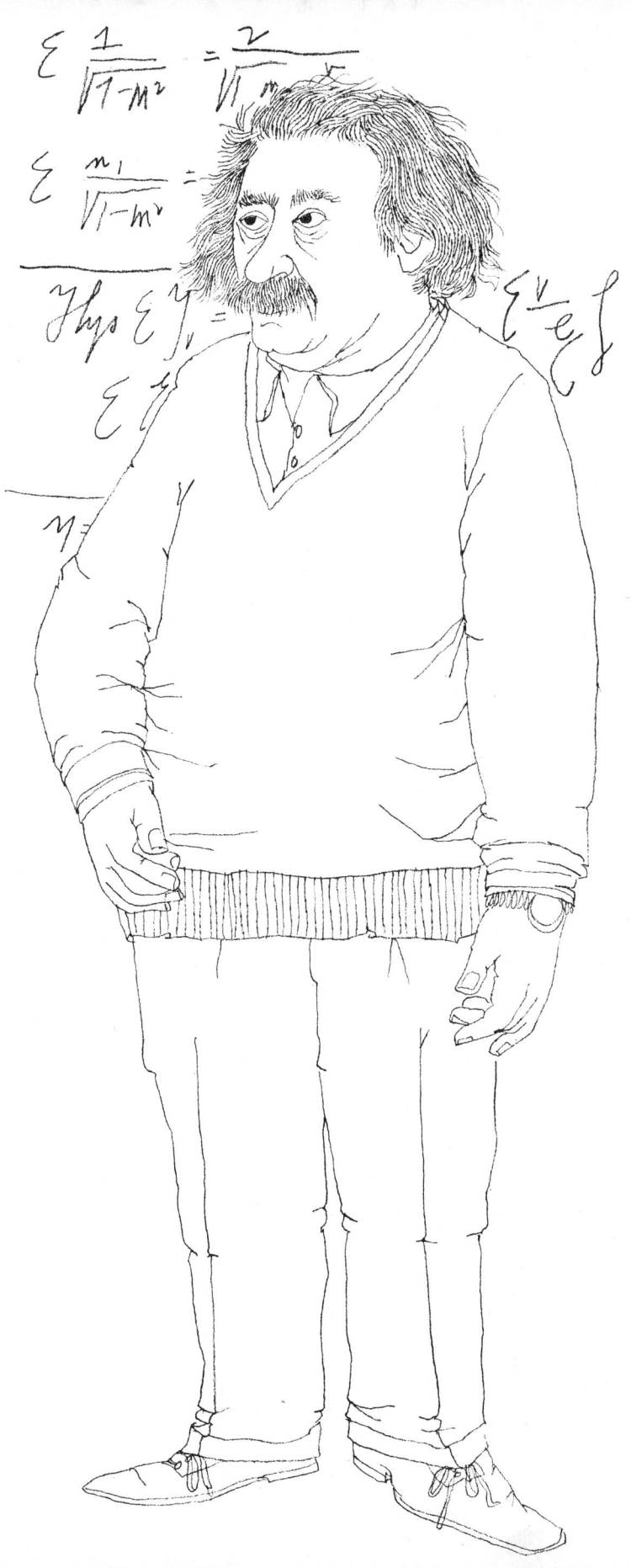

17
St. Patrick's Day

This is a holiday for the Irish who wear a sprig of shamrock, their three-leaf emblem, to mark it. St. Patrick, the patron saint of Ireland, was British by birth.

THE ORIGINAL ROBINSON CRUSOE

Daniel Defoe modeled his Robinson Crusoe on a Scottish sailor called Alexander Selkirk. Selkirk was sailing in the Pacific on a privateering expedition. He quarreled with his captain who marooned him on Juan Fernandez Island off the coast of Chile. Selkirk managed to survive for almost five years before another privateer stopped and rescued him.

MARCH

21
Vernal Equinox

'Vernal' means 'spring,' and 'equinox' means 'equal night.' This is the day in spring when the sun moves so that the day and the night are equal in length all over the earth.

The sun now enters the sign of Aries the Ram, through which it goes until April 20.

The shortest people and the tallest people are both Negro. The shortest people are the Pygmies; the average height for men is under 4 feet 9 inches. The tallest people are the Nilotics; the men average over 7 feet.

JEREMY CRABAPPLE says:

*Hard to study when young,
harder to be ignorant when old.*

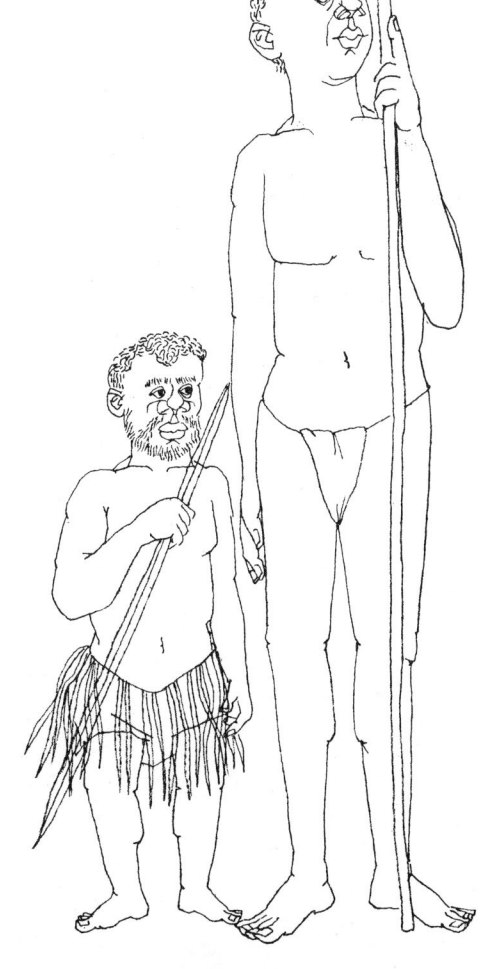

APRIL

The name comes from a Latin word meaning 'to open.'
And it is a time of opening.
The buds open, and the earth grows green with leaves and grasses.
Even people come out of their winter clothes.
For the ancient Romans the month was sacred to Venus,
their goddess of love.
Love shows itself on all sides at this time,
in bird and beast.

APRIL

1
All Fools' Day

This is the day to be on guard against people who play jokes. A good joke is worth a good laugh, and nobody minds the cry of 'April fool!' The real April fool is anybody who thinks a rude trick is funny.

2
BIRTHDAY OF
Hans Christian Andersen 1805

Andersen was a person as odd as some of the characters in his own fairy tales. His father was a poor shoemaker. Father, mother and child lived in one room. When he was eleven his father died. Hans stopped going to school and stayed at home. He played with a toy theater, and spent his time making clothes for the puppets and reading all the plays he could lay his hands on. At fourteen he ran off to Copenhagen to become an opera singer. He nearly starved until he made friends with two musicians who helped him. His voice gave out, he turned to dancing and was admitted by the Royal Theater as a pupil. He did not study as he should, and his friends lost interest in him. Luckily he made a new friend, Jonas Collin, the director of the Royal Theater.

Collin sent Andersen, who was now seventeen, to school. Just before leaving, he published his first book, but it had no success. The five years he spent in school were the unhappiest in his life. He was almost fully a man, queer, tall and awkward, and he had to sit with little boys to make up for the time he had lost. At last Collin agreed that Andersen had enough schooling, and Andersen came back to Copenhagen. He set to work writing and

APRIL

began to publish book after book: poems, novels, plays, travel books. By the time he was thirty he had gained some reputation as a writer.

At this time he published a little book of fairy tales that did not attract much notice. Andersen himself had no notion that this was the beginning of his real fame. He kept on working away at plays, novels and travel books. But every year he would write and publish a few fairy tales. Little by little their fame spread, and translations in many languages were published. All his life Andersen kept trying to make a success in the theater. But his plays were not very good. It was not until late in life that Andersen realized that his fairy tales were his chief claim to fame.

Andersen's way of telling a story brings it to life in every little incident. Everything takes on the color of his own personality. Sometimes he is funny and sometimes he is sad. But there is always a touch of humor in his sadness, and something sad hiding behind his humor.

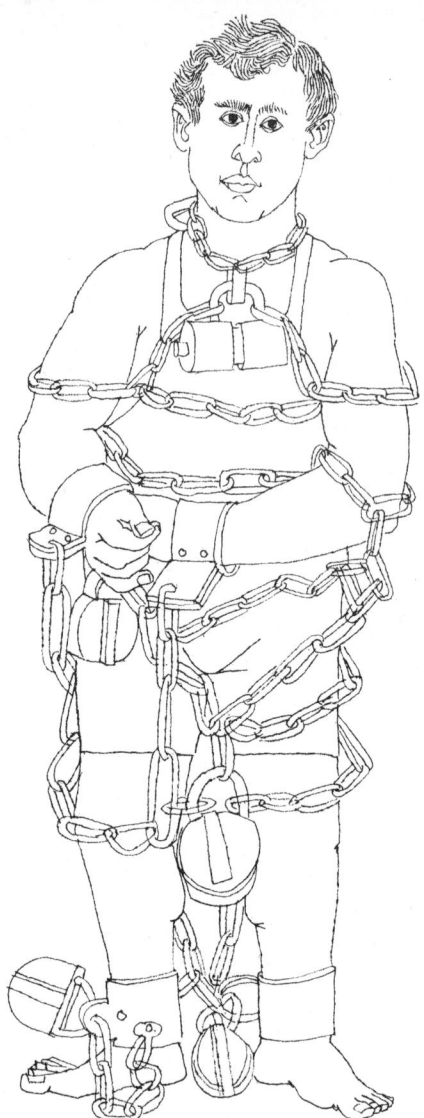

6
BIRTHDAY OF
Harry Houdini 1874

His real name was Weiss. He took the name 'Houdini' because he admired the great French magician, Houdin. Houdini was the most famous magician of his time, and he invented many remarkable tricks. His greatest reputation was as an escape artist. He managed to escape from what seemed hopeless traps. He would let himself be tied and chained inside a large box. The box would be lowered from a bridge into a river. In a few minutes Houdini would pop out of the water, and swim to safety.

These escapes were pretty dangerous. They depended not only on trickery, but on strength, speed and agility. The books he wrote about his experiences make interesting reading.

APRIL

6
First Visit to the North Pole ₁₉₀₉

The first men to reach the North Pole were of the three main races of man. The party was led by Commodore Robert E. Peary, a white man. The others were Matthew Henson, a Negro, and four Eskimos. They stayed at the Pole for thirty-six hours.

The main source of chicle is the sap of the sapodilla tree which grows in Guatemala, British Honduras and Mexico. Chicle is needed for dental supplies, but its principal use is in making chewing gum.

STAMPS

The first postage stamps in the world were the penny and two-penny stamps issued in 1840 by the British Postal Service. People began collecting them at once. By 1860 collectors had begun to pay attention to paper, watermarks, perforations, color shade and outline. And they soon were collecting 'entires,' envelopes and postcards with the stamps on them. The number of issued stamps has grown so large that most serious collectors specialize in particular countries or areas. There are several stamps of which only a single specimen survives. The most famous of these is the British Guiana 1c black on magenta of 1856, which some think the most valuable stamp in the world. It was originally bought from a schoolboy for $1.20.

The ancient Egyptians used lead for writing on papyrus, and the Romans also knew that lead made marks on paper and used it for writing. Our so-called lead pencil, however, has no lead in it at all. The substance that does the writing is a mixture of graphite and pipe clay. A hard pencil has more clay in it, a soft pencil more graphite. The reason for the word 'lead' in the pencil's name is that when graphite was first discovered and used instead of lead because it made a darker mark, it was called 'black lead.'

APRIL

8
The Buddha

This day is a Buddhist holiday, because it is held to be the day on which Buddha, the founder of Buddhism, was born, more than twenty-five hundred years ago.

Buddha was a prince who spent the first years of his life in luxury. At the age of twenty-nine he first became aware of human misery and eager to understand the meaning of life. He left his wife and children, and gave up his wealth and position. He studied under several teachers, but could learn nothing that would satisfy him. He went into the wilderness, and for six years starved and tortured himself, but still remained in doubt. Giving up his harsh life, he sat down under a large fig tree and thought for a long time. At last he had a vision which gave the answer to all his doubts. From this time on until his death at the age of eighty he went about teaching and persuading others to believe as he did.

The main idea of Buddhism is that all suffering is caused by desire, and the way to get rid of suffering is to get rid of all desire. This is very hard to do; Buddhism teaches how to do it little by little. Buddhists also believe that everybody is born and dies many times. If a person lives rightly, he will be better in his next life. If he behaves wrongly, his next life will be worse, and he may even be changed into an animal.

Hundreds of millions of people, mostly in Asia, are followers of the Buddha today.

8
Fountain of Youth 1513

The Spanish explorer, Ponce de Leon, looking for the Fountain of Youth, landed in Florida on this day.

APRIL

13

BIRTHDAY OF

Thomas Jefferson 1743

The basic ideas of Jefferson are now so much a part of American life that it is hard to realize that he had to struggle to get them tried. Although well-to-do and of an upper-class family, he was a complete democrat. He believed that every man should have a vote, and that free public education for all would prepare people to vote wisely. He believed in freedom of religion, and he tried to free the slaves. He wanted all men to have an equal chance, with no special privileges for anybody.

As a man it would be hard to find his equal. He was about six feet tall, slim, erect and strong, with sandy hair and gray eyes. He was not handsome, but strong-looking. He was a fine horseman and skillful at outdoor sports. He was a good singer and dancer, and played the violin well. When he graduated from William and Mary College at twenty he knew Latin, Greek and French, and was well-versed, for his time, in higher mathematics and natural science. Soon after he learned Spanish, Italian and Anglo-Saxon. He remained a serious student all his life. A few of the studies he became expert in are: agriculture, botany, architecture, geology, geography, ethnology, medicine, surgery, law, government, religion, literature and zoology. He not only studied these fields; he did practical work in them as well, some of it of importance. In character he was remarkably well-balanced. He was kind-hearted and even-tempered, frank, honest and firm. He never argued and he did not hold a grudge. He treated all men as his equals.

What Jefferson himself thought the most important things he had done may be seen in the epitaph he wrote for his gravestone. 'Here was buried Thomas Jefferson, author of the Declaration of American Independence, of the statute of Virginia for religious freedom, and father of the University of Virginia.'

Peanut oil is used for many purposes. The strangest use of all, though, is for underwater cooking in submarines. The undersea fleet like it because it does not smoke unless heated above 450 degrees F.

APRIL

18
San Francisco Earthquake ₁₉₀₆

This great earthquake caused the San Francisco fire. The ground was torn open for a length of two hundred and seventy miles. Between them, the earthquake and the fire killed about seven hundred people and caused damage estimated at one hundred and forty million dollars.

The old woman who lived in a shoe and had so many children she didn't know what to do was just an amateur. A Russian woman, Mrs. Fedor Vassilef, had 69 children. She had 16 sets of twins, 7 sets of triplets and 4 sets of quadruplets.

20
Taurus

The sign of Taurus, the Bull, begins now and lasts until May 21.

23
BIRTHDAY OF
William
Shakespeare 1564

Shakespeare is the greatest of English poets and dramatists. Most poets have thought well of their own work, and many have said it. But in Shakespeare's case it was no vain boast when he wrote:

Not marble, nor the gilded monuments
Of princes, shall outlive this powerful rhyme

29
Arbor Day

This is the day to think about trees; the many uses they have, and the great pleasure they give us. Plant a tree, whenever you have a chance. Men have cut down and burned down too much. The earth is crowded with deserts, dust bowls and stone cities. Let's make it green again.

APRIL

30
Death of Bayard 1524

On this day died in battle one of the noblest knights of all time, Pierre Terrail de Bayard. He was known as the 'knight without fear and fault' because of his courage and skill in war, and his loyalty and unselfishness. He was also called 'the good knight' because of his kindness. He fought in defense of his country, France, and received every honor from his countrymen. He was killed at 51 while defending the rear of the French army in retreat.

At one time pens were made out of the quills of bird's feathers. To write properly, the quill had to be sharpened, and scribes carried a small knife to keep their pens sharp. We still call the small knife a 'penknife.'

April is a good time to get acquainted with the early flowers. Flowers start at different times, depending on how far north or south you live, but by April the early flowers are out even pretty far north. All plants like to grow in special places, and there are three main kinds of places they like. The water-loving plants grow in swamps, beside streams, and around the shores of ponds and lakes. The plants that like a medium amount of water around their roots grow in woods where the soil keeps fairly moist. And last, there are the field plants that like the dry sunny places.

Here are a few flowers from each kind of place. Jack in the Pulpit, a greenish brown flower, likes the high part of wet ground, and is out by April. In the lower wetter ground you will find the blue flowers, the Violet and the Blue Flag or Iris, which come out later. The hardest to find is the Forget-me-not, which grows around the edge of little brooks.

In the woods there are many more flowers, so start by learning just a few. The Red Trillium or Wake Robin starts blooming in April and keeps going through May. The Columbine, has little red and yellow bells for flowers, and comes out a little later. Then there are the White, the Blue and the Yellow Violet, all different and all related to the Violet of the swamp.

Of the field flowers a good one is the Wild Strawberry which has a triple leaf and a white flower. The commonest yellow flower is the Five Finger or Cinquefoil. It gets its name from its bunch of five leaves. The little flower looks almost like a very small buttercup. The earliest blue flower of the field is the bluet, a tiny four-petalled flower. Wherever you find it the field is full of it.

JEREMY CRABAPPLE *says:*

A monkey in full dress
Is a monkey no less.

MAY

May was named after Maia, a Roman goddess of Spring.
In many places the countryside is at its best at this time.
The flowers are still in their early freshness.
The birds have come back
from their winter stay in the south,
and fill the air with song.
If only the world were properly run,
this would be the time to shut up school and start vacations.

MAY

1
May Day

In olden times everybody used to get up at dawn and go a-Maying to the woods. They would come back in a parade, carrying flowers and branches of trees. The *maypole*, covered with ribbons and wreaths, would be carried in the center, and set up in the village square. The whole day and most of the night would be spent in sport and jollity, with dancing around the maypole and good things to eat and drink.

MAYDAY, the call for help used by ships and planes in trouble has nothing to do with May Day. It's just an English spelling of the way the French word 'm'aidez' sounds. 'M'aidez' means 'help me.'

Mother's Day

The second Sunday in May is the day picked to honor mothers. Everybody is supposed to do something special for his mother. The thing mothers like best is to know their children want to please them. Every day in the year is a good day to think of mother, but for those who have forgotten, Mother's Day is the time to start right again.

12
BIRTHDAY OF
Edward Lear 1812

The inventor of the limerick and author of the Nonsense Books was born in London. He began to draw as a child. He liked music and had some talent for it, and he liked to write and had some talent for that. But, best of all, he liked to draw, and especially to draw birds.

When he was twenty he published some pictures of rare parrots. The Earl of Derby saw the pictures and thought they were very good. The Earl had a menagerie of his own, and he engaged Lear to paint pictures of the animals.

MAY

Lear had a way of talking that was very funny, and the whole family of the Earl became his friends. And he created his first Nonsense Book to amuse Edward, the grandson of the Earl.

Later Lear moved to Italy. He spent much of his long life travelling and writing books about his travels, which he illustrated with pictures of the interesting places he saw.

Although he was a good painter, especially in his small pictures and sketches, his fame is based on his Nonsense Books, which are the best things of their kind in the English language. If you understand how to read nonsense —for nonsense makes a good deal of sense when it is properly read—you will get a good idea of what Lear was like from a poem about himself that begins:

'How pleasant to know Mr. Lear!
    Who has written such volumes of stuff!
Some think him ill-tempered and queer,
    But a few think him pleasant enough.
His mind is concrete and fastidious,
    His nose is remarkably big;
His visage is more or less hideous,
    His beard it resembles a wig.
He has ears, and two eyes, and ten fingers,
    Leastways if you reckon two thumbs;
Long ago he was one of the singers,
    But now he is one of the dumbs.'

MAY

19
BIRTHDAY OF
Nellie Melba ₁₈₅₉

One of the greatest singers in the world, she was born near Melbourne in Australia, and her real name was Helen Porter Mitchell. She took 'Melba' for her singing name from Melbourne, the city where she started. She showed her talent for music and her beautiful voice early in life. She sang in public for the first time at the age of six. Her father was fairly well-to-do and could afford to give her a good musical education. And she was lucky, also, that there were good teachers near her home. She learned to sing easily and well, to play the piano, and to understand music. She went to Europe for her final studies.

She did not sing in opera until she was completely ready. She was twenty-eight before she made her debut in the role of 'Lucia.' She was at once successful, and from that time on sang in all the great opera houses of the world. She became so famous that restaurants gave her name to the foods she liked to eat, and we still call the thin dry pieces of toast 'Melba toast' and a dessert 'peach Melba.'

She made a great many records, and they are well worth listening to. Her singing comes near to perfection. Her voice was clear and had a lovely sound, whether high or low. And it moved from tone to tone cleanly and quickly. Even when she was past sixty her voice sounded like that of a young girl. Besides singing difficult pieces from opera in which her voice leaped about like a flute, she also sang simple songs well. One of her favorite songs was 'Home, Sweet Home,' and she has left us a record of it.

21
First Solo Flight Across the Atlantic 1927

One of the great moments in the development of aviation was the first one-man flight across the Atlantic. Charles Lindbergh started from New York on May 20, 1927 and thirty-three and a half hours later landed the Spirit of St. Louis in Paris. Overnight an unknown flyer became an international hero. The record doesn't look like much now, but considering the kind of plane he had, Lindbergh's was a remarkable feat.

21
Gemini

On this day, the sun enters the sign of Gemini, the Twins, and stays in this area of the Zodiac until June 21.

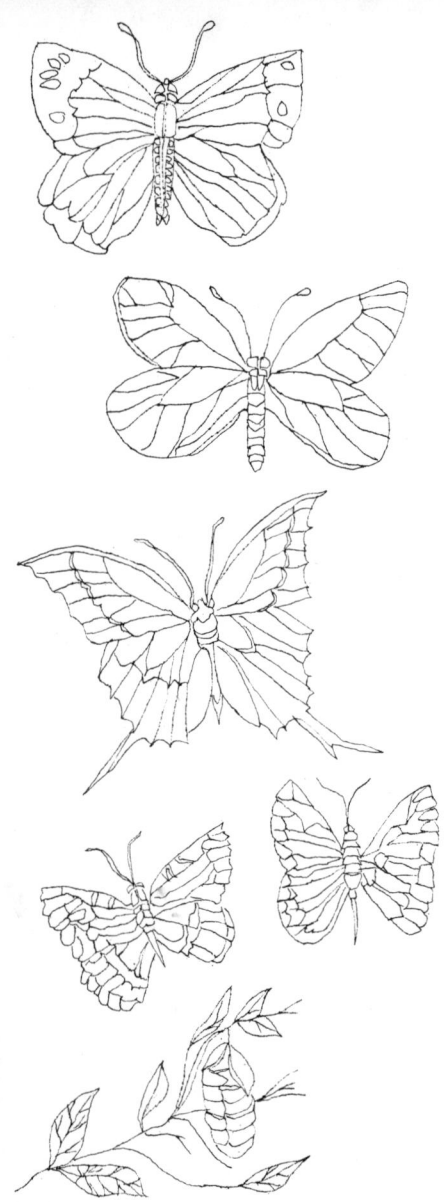

THE LIFE OF THE BUTTERFLY

May is the time we begin to see many butterflies in the fields. The butterfly has a strange life. Most animals are born looking much the same as they do for the rest of their lives, only smaller. But what we call the butterfly never grows. It is the last stage of a life that has gone through different forms. The first form is the egg. Late in summer or early in the fall, if you look around, you can find the tiny eggs on the under side of leaves or stuck to a small twig. The mother always lays them close to the food they will need to eat when they are hatched. As soon as the eggs are laid, the first changes begin inside the thin shell. Little by little the soft inside turns into a little animal like a worm. And finally, when complete, it becomes a caterpillar. The caterpillar may be hatched in spring or late summer or fall, depending on the kind of butterfly it is.

For two or three months the caterpillar does nothing but eat and grow. As it gets bigger, it sheds its skin four or five times. Its body is made up of thirteen parts, each one of them like a tiny blown-up automobile tube. The three parts behind the small head have a pair of legs each, like the three pairs of legs of the butterfly. The rest of it is all stomach, demanding to be filled.

After this long period of eating and growing the caterpillar becomes sleepy. It attaches itself by its tail to a stick or a stone or the under side of a branch, and curls up. As it sleeps, a hard coat forms on its shrunken body. The caterpillar has begun to go into its next change. The thirteen parts of the caterpillar are turning into a tight little body with big delicate wings like gauze, and long feelers.

One day the hard coat breaks open, and a little

wet insect crawls out. A few hours in the sun and the butterfly has become itself.

Most butterflies spend the winter sleeping, either as eggs or in the hard shell. But some of them don't. You can sometimes see a butterfly in the winter, fluttering from tree to tree. It is the mourning-cloak butterfly which hides all winter in sheltered places, emerging now and then, when the weather turns mild. Some butterflies even go south in the winter, like migrating birds. The Monarch, a big red-brown butterfly, gathers in large flocks in the fall. They fly south for hundreds of miles. The butterflies called 'painted ladies' pass the winter in the North African desert. In spring they fly north over the Mediterranean Sea, some of them reaching as far as Iceland. The butterfly you look at in May might be just born, or might have spent the winter in the woods, or might have just arrived from its southern winter quarters.

30
Memorial Day

This day is dedicated to the memory of all who died in war for the United States.

> *How sleep the brave, who sink to rest,*
> *By all their country's wishes blest!*
> *When Spring, with dewy fingers cold,*
> *Returns to deck their hallow'd mold,*
> *She there shall dress a sweeter sod*
> *Than Fancy's feet have ever trod.*
>
> *By fairy hands their knell is rung,*
> *By forms unseen their dirge is sung;*
> *There Honour comes, a pilgrim gray,*
> *To bless the turf that wraps their clay,*
> *And Freedom shall awhile repair*
> *To dwell, a weeping hermit, there!*

WILLIAM COLLINS

HALLEY'S COMET

The first man to figure out the movement of a comet, and to predict when it would return, was Edmund Halley, a friend of Sir Isaac Newton and a great astronomer. Halley saw the comet in 1682, and decided that it was the same one that had been seen in 1531 and 1607. He predicted that it would return in 1757, and came pretty close to the right date, for the comet showed up in 1759. Halley's comet—it has been named after him—made its last appearance in 1910. It is thought that the earth passed through its tail in May, 1910. If you can wait until 1986, you will be able to see Halley's comet; that will be its next appearance.

HUNDRED YARD DASH

If you want to break the world's record in the hundred yard dash, May seems to be the month to try it. The present record is 9.3 seconds, and it has been made nine times. Five of the nine were in the month of May, the others in March, April and June. It would also be a good idea to try it in California, as the record was made in California and three others who tied it also ran in California.

MAY

*P*lants are not as innocent as they look. There are some 400 species of meat-eating plants. Of these the best known American kind is the pitcher plant. Its leaf, shaped like a small cream pitcher, attracts insects. Once inside they have little chance of climbing out. The walls are steep and smooth, and near the top have long stiff hairs pointing downward. When the tired insect drops to the bottom, it drowns in the pool of water there, and is slowly absorbed by the hungry plant.

JEREMY CRABAPPLE says:

Nobody ever wore out his face washing it.

JUNE

June is the first month of Summer.
Gardens now come into flower.
It is the favorite time for weddings, and also for voyages.
Best of all, it is the month when schools close.
The name comes to us from the ancient Romans,
but we are not sure what they named it for.
Perhaps they named it for the Goddess Juno
who was the guardian of weddings.

JUNE

2

BIRTHDAY OF

Thomas Hardy ₁₈₄₀

He began as an architect, turned to writing novels, and in his later years devoted himself to poetry. His many novels and poems are sad because Hardy sees the world as ruled by chance. Every effort is doomed to failure at the end. The best thing to do is endure whatever happens with patience. Here is a poem of his that is worth remembering.

WAITING BOTH

A star looks down at me,
And says: 'Here I and you
Stand each in our degree:
What do you mean to do,—
    Mean to do?'
I say: 'For all I know,
Wait, and let Time go by,
Till my change come.'—'Just so,'
The star says: 'So mean I:—
    So mean I.'

JUNE

6
The Year Without a Summer ₁₈₁₆

The weather takes queer turns at times, as you know. This was one long remembered in New England, and not a pleasant memory either. Who could expect snow at this time of the year, but on this day snow fell and a frost set in. Crops were destroyed. By the fall, food was scarce. Wild animals, domestic animals and people, all suffered. The year was properly called the 'starving year,' as well as the 'year without a summer.'

7
Death of Mohammed ₆₃₂

Mohammed, the founder of one of the world's great religions, was born about 570 A.D. in Mecca. His father who was poor died when he was born. His mother gave him to a Bedouin nurse to be brought up in the desert. After three years the Bedouins returned the child because he was subject to fits and the Bedouins thought there were devils in him. After the death of his mother Mohammed was brought up first by his grandfather and then by his uncle who took him on long caravan journeys through Arabia and Syria. At 25 Mohammed went to work for a rich widow and soon married her, although she was about 15 years older. He took charge of her business affairs, and became known as an honest and shrewd businessman.

From childhood Mohammed had thought about religion. As he grew older he took to spending a month alone on a mountain near Mecca. When he was forty he announced that he was a prophet and that the angel Gabriel had given him the word of God. This he set down in the Koran, which became the bible of the new religion. At first Mohammed had trouble in spreading his beliefs. His preaching against idols made him unpopular and he had to leave Mecca for a while to save his life.

The first big step forward came in the year 622, when Mohammed moved to another city with a band of followers. This flight from Mecca is called the "Hegira." The city they went to took the name "Medina," which means "city of the prophet." The date of the Hegira is reckoned as the beginning of the Mohammedan calendar. From the Hegira on Mohammedanism spread more rapidly. As he became more powerful Mohammed began to wage war to spread his religion. After his death Mohammedanism spread through many parts of Asia and Africa, and at one time came close to conquering Europe.

We call the religion, "Mohammedanism" after its founder. Its followers call it "Islam," which means "accepting one's fate." Some of the basic beliefs Mohammed took from the Hebrew Bible, and he combined them with local Arab beliefs in fairies, genii and giants. All believers have to pray five times a day facing Mecca. They have to wash, take off their shoes and kneel in a clean place while praying. They have also to make a pilgrimage to Mecca, to fast during the month of Ramadan, and give money regularly to charity. They are permitted to take more than one wife, but in fact they rarely do. The Koran forbids drinking intoxicating liquors, gambling, charging interest on a loan and making an image of any creature, man or animal. Mohammedans who kill an unbeliever will be rewarded in Paradise, and those who are killed by unbelievers are regarded as martyrs.

JUNE

8
BIRTHDAY OF
Frank Lloyd Wright ₁₈₆₉

Some people like the Guggenheim Museum in New York very much and some don't like it at all. Like most of Wright's buildings it arouses strong feelings one way or the other, because it is so individual, so different from other things. But no matter how people feel about any particular building that Wright designed, most of them agree that he is the most original architect of our time, one of the most remarkable of all time, and certainly the greatest American architect.

He was the pupil and later the assistant of Louis Sullivan, another great American architect. From Sullivan he learned one important thing: the form of a building should depend on what it is used for. Starting with this basic idea, he added to it two other ideas of his own; that the plan of a building should grow out of the needs of the people for whom it is designed, and that a building should fit into the landscape around it. He built houses to suit the flat prairie, the bare desert, the sides of hills, even one to go with a waterfall.

Wright was a man of tremendous energy and will. He was always ready to try something new and to take risks. He was not discouraged when he ran into difficulties. He fought back when he was attacked. Until the very end of his long life he kept trying to make buildings that were new in design and better fitted to the needs of our time. His last work was the Guggenheim Museum.

JUNE

CROCODILE TEARS

Where do people get the notion that a crocodile pretends to weep for his victim, so that 'crocodile tears' means 'making a pretense of being sorry for somebody?' The idea comes from a simple fact. When a crocodile opens his jaws very wide to get something large into his mouth, his eyes water. In the same way our own eyes water when we yawn.

14
Flag Day *1777*

On this day the Continental Congress adopted a design for a flag, which is the basis of all later American flags: thirteen stars and stripes, one for each of the original states. In 1794 Congress voted to add two stripes and two stars to the flag, because Vermont and Kentucky had been added to the Union. By 1818 there were twenty states in the Union. Seeing that the flag would become too cluttered, Congress voted to return to the original thirteen stripes, and to add one star for each new state on the July 4 after its admission. On July 4, 1959 the forty-ninth star was added for Alaska, and on July 4, 1960 the fiftieth star for Hawaii.

16
Naming of America *1497*

Amerigo Vespucci, an Italian navigator in the employ of Spain, claimed that he had touched the mainland of America on this day. This made him the first European to reach the mainland of the new world, and 'America' was named after him. Recent studies have cast doubt on Vespucci's claim. It may be that John Cabot, an Italian navigator sailing under English colors, was actually the first, on June 24, 1497. Would America have been the same if it had been named Johnsland?

17 Battle of Bunker Hill 1775

The first big battle of the American Revolution is so called, although it was actually fought on Breed's Hill nearby. The British were besieged in Boston. To prevent them from taking the heights around Boston, the Committee of Safety sent William Prescott and 2500 men to fortify Bunker Hill. Instead Prescott chose Breed's Hill, which was nearer Boston and more exposed. The British under General Howe charged up the hill twice. The Americans did not fire until they were thirty yards away. In the second charge the American ammunition gave out and the British took the hill. The British lost 1054 men, the Americans 449. Though they lost the battle, the Americans were inspired by the brave defense. How often has it been true that the side that loses the first battle wins the war!

The use of homing pigeons to carry messages is very old, going back to ancient Persia. The Greeks used homing pigeons to carry back the names of Olympic winners to their home cities.

The first time a pigeon flew 500 miles in one day was June 30, 1896. It made the distance in just over ten hours. The longest flight made by a pigeon began on June 1, 1845. It was released from a sailing ship off the Ichibo Islands, West Africa. Fifty-five days later it dropped dead just a mile short of its home loft in London. It had gone a distance of 5,400 miles by airline route. Its actual flight was probably 7,000 miles, to get around the Sahara Desert.

Father's Day

The third Sunday in June is the day to do something special for father.

21
Summer Solstice

This is the day when the sun is highest in the sky at noon, and the longest day of the year between sunrise and sunset. The sun now enters the sign of Cancer, the Crab, where it remains until July 20.

JUNE

25

A Great Beginning 1886

The Rossi Grand Opera Company was touring in South America. On this evening they were getting ready to start a performance of 'Aida,' but the conductor was missing. At the last minute a substitute was found. The first cellist of the orchestra, who was nineteen years old, came to the stand. It was the first time he had ever conducted. He conducted the entire opera from memory. The performance was a success, and the young conductor highly praised.

In this dramatic way began the career of the most famous conductor of recent times, Arturo Toscanini. In a few years he became conductor of La Scala, the most important opera house in Italy. From La Scala he went to the Metropolitan Opera House in New York. After many years of conducting opera he became conductor of the Philharmonic Symphony orchestra of New York, and devoted himself to symphonic music. In old age he turned to radio, and directed the N.B.C. Symphony orchestra. On April 14, 1954, ten days after his eighty-seventh birthday, he conducted the N.B.C. Symphony orchestra in Carnegie Hall for the last time. Thus ended the longest and most brilliant career in the history of conducting: sixty-eight years of untiring devotion to music.

JUNE

29
BIRTHDAY OF
Peter Paul Rubens 1577

Most great artists had difficult lives. They had to struggle against obstacles of every kind. They suffered as much as they achieved. Some of them died in poverty, and their fame did not begin to spread until after their death. Rubens is the one example of a great artist who was the favorite of good fortune all his life.

Rubens was a man of great strength, energy and brilliance of mind. He was handsome, charming, made friends easily and was admired by everybody who knew him. He was well-educated and had a good command of Latin, French, Italian, Spanish, German, Dutch and English. His mother did not stand in his way when he wished to become a painter. He was apprenticed to good teachers and he became a master at the age of twenty-one. In his thirties he was known throughout Europe as a great painter. His pictures brought very high prices, and he became rich. He had dozens of pupils and assistants who were eager to help him and learn from him. The kings and nobles for whom he painted many of his pictures saw his ability not only as a painter but as a man of affairs. They employed him as an ambassador between nations. While painting his pictures he arranged treaties and smoothed out differences between the most powerful rulers of the times.

Rubens loved to paint works of the largest size. His best pictures are huge canvasses with dozens of figures on them. His painting is vigorous, rich in color and grand in conception.

Rubens was even fortunate in his death. He died at the height of his fame and powers. His last works show no sign of old age or of any falling off of skill and imagination.

JUNE

ROWING THE ATLANTIC

If you haven't a sail or a motor or a tow, rowing is a good way of moving a boat across the water. But who would think of trying to row a boat across the Atlantic Ocean? Two men did. On June 6, 1897 George Haroo and Frank Samuelson left New York in an eighteen-foot boat, without mast or sails. All they carried to move the boat was five pairs of oars. Fifty-five days later they landed on the Scilly Isles off the coast of England. They had rowed at least 3,075 miles.

Why does a cat purr? Because it's happy. How does a cat purr? Nobody really knows. The one thing that is certain is that a cat keeps purring both when breathing in and breathing out.

TIGHTROPE WALKERS

The greatest tightrope walker of all time was the Frenchman, Blondin. He made the first crossing of Niagara Falls on a rope 1100 feet long and 160 feet above the Falls on June 30, 1859. But it was during the following July that he did his most amazing feats, crossing the Falls many times: blindfolded, in a sack, pushing a wheelbarrow, carrying a man on his back, sitting down in the middle of the rope while he cooked and ate an omelette. Blondin had an astounding career. He made his first appearance as a circus acrobat at the age of six. He gave his last performance as a tightrope walker at the age of seventy-two.

THE FAMILY OF THE ROSE

The wild roses and the garden roses are both in bloom in June. And we see many other flowers on trees and bushes and creepers that seem to be like roses. In fact there are hundreds of plants of the rose family. The rose family has not only given us many beautiful and sweet-smelling flowers. It has given us some of our best fruits. Among the fruits of the rose family are apple, cherry, pear, plum, peach, strawberry, raspberry, blackberry and almond. These fruits were not as delicious as they are today when they first appeared

JUNE

in wild plants. They were cultivated and improved by men, beginning way back in the New Stone Age, about eight thousand years ago. One branch of the rose family, that of the almond, peach, plum and apricot, began in Turkestan. The one that includes the apple, pear, cherry and quince probably was first cultivated in the neighborhood of Iran.

For hundreds of years, birds have been kept as pets in China. Nowadays, more than fifty different kinds of birds are caged and tamed, some for their song, some for their looks, and some because they can be taught to do tricks.

JEREMY CRABAPPLE says:

Most people find it easier to swim in shallow water.

JULY

July is the hot month.
In the heat of day
older folks cling to the shade,
but boys and girls run about under the sun,
as happy as grasshoppers.
The Romans named the month
in honor of Julius Caesar
who was born on July 12, 100 B.C.

JULY

1
Dominion Day

In 1867 the provinces of Canada united to form the Dominion of Canada. The day of the act has been celebrated ever since as a Canadian holiday. The flag is flown, and the Canadian anthem, 'The Maple Leaf Forever,' is sung.

3
The Dog Days

The time called the 'dog days' begins now and lasts until August 11. The dog of the name is Sirius, the Dog Star, which rises with the sun during this period. It is a popular notion that this is the hottest and muggiest part of the year, and this is often true. There is no truth, however, in the superstition that dogs are likely to go mad from the heat.

Most of our sugar is crystals formed from the juice of either the sugar cane or the sugar beet. In Burma, however, they make sugar, very much like our maple sugar, out of the sap of the toddy palm, a large palm tree.

THE FIRST MONEY

Trade was first carried on by barter, by swapping one thing for another. Then people used precious metals, weighing out the proper quantity to pay for a purchase. In the Iron Age, just over four thousand years ago, the Lydians of Asia Minor invented money. They made coins which contained a fixed weight of gold or silver, and saved the trouble of weighing out the metal for every sale. The Chinese, in the seventh century, were the first to make use of paper money.

JULY

4
Independence Day

The Declaration of Independence was adopted on this day in 1776. Ever since, the Fourth of July has been celebrated as the day of the founding of the United States, with speeches and with fireworks.

Two of the greatest founding fathers, Thomas Jefferson and John Adams, died at almost the same moment on July 4, 1826. Jefferson was eighty-three, Adams was ninety-one; their acts and thoughts were noble to the end.

7
BIRTHDAY OF
Pinocchio

In 1881 Carlo Lorenzini, an Italian writer, using the pen name 'Collodi,' published a story about a wooden puppet called Pinocchio. Since then 'The Adventures of Pinocchio' has gone around the world, and is a favorite book with children everywhere. Pinocchio is as real as a person. He is conceited, careless, more than a little bad, and yet likable. His adventures are funny and at the same time moving.

JULY

8
BIRTHDAY OF
Jean de la Fontaine
1621

A fable is a little story in which animals, and even sometimes trees and stones and other things in nature, talk as if they were human. What happens leads up to a moral, which is the point of the whole story. Fables were told thousands of years ago. The earliest book of them, the 'Panchatranta,' was written in India more than two thousand years ago. And a slave, Aesop, became famous in ancient Greece for the fables he told. Many writers in many countries have written fables since then, but one man wrote them so well that his fables are the best liked in the world. He was the French poet, La Fontaine.

La Fontaine invented few of his fables. Most of the stories he took from earlier writers. But the way he told them made all the difference. The poetry moves with a lively rhythm, and the words are fitted together very smoothly. The animals and other characters talk like real people. La Fontaine is full of sly humor. He makes fun of everything and everybody, but he does it so kindly that no one can take offense. And sometimes the story is sad, and the reader is moved by La Fontaine's tenderness and gentle sympathy.

French boys and girls learn many of his fables by heart. If you ever study French, you will do so too. It's worth studying French just for the pleasure of reading La Fontaine in the original version.

14 Bastille Day

The fourteenth of July is the great national holiday of France. It dates from the storming of the Bastille on July 14, 1789, the riot that started the French Revolution. The Bastille was an old fortress that was used as a prison for political prisoners, as well as for criminals. The Paris mob broke in, killed the governor and freed a few prisoners. The Revolution that grew out of this riot ended the French monarchy and ultimately led to the present democratic government of France.

15 St. Swithin's Day

There is an old English legend that, if it rains on St. Swithin's Day, it will keep raining for forty days, if not, it will stay fair for forty days. The story goes that St. Swithin was buried by his own request in the churchyard of Winchester Cathedral. When he was made a saint, the monks decided to move his body into the Cathedral. On the day planned, the fifteenth of July, it rained heavily and kept raining for the next forty days. This made people believe that St. Swithin preferred staying out in the open. There are similar stories for other saints in France and Holland.

JULY

15
BIRTHDAY OF
Rembrandt Van Rijn 1606

The fifteenth of July is worth remembering also as the birthday of one of the greatest artists in the world. Rembrandt was born in the great time of Holland when the country became rich and produced many famous men. Rembrandt is the most famous of all. He is one of the greatest portrait painters of all time. He brings together realism, a poetic imagination, great insight into character, and every skill a painter can have. He is the best etcher of all time. No other artist comes near the variety of his work in this medium, and few touch at any point the heights he reached in every kind of etching.

Not much is known of his youth. His family was prosperous, and he was sent to a good school. He left to be apprenticed to a painter. He worked hard at his studies, spending all his spare time in making sketches of people. He was successful while still young, and became the leading painter in Holland. Although he was rich and enjoyed the good things of life, painting remained his main passion. As he grew older, his luck changed. He lost his money. His paintings lost their popularity, and the fickle public turned to new artists who were much inferior to him. Still, he kept painting until the end of his life, doing some of his best pictures in his last years.

Rembrandt painted about seven hundred pictures. Among the most interesting are his self-portraits, painted at various times in his life from youth to old age.

JULY

17
First Atom Bomb $_{1945}$

The first atom bomb was exploded on this day at Alamogordo, New Mexico. Perhaps this was the beginning of a new age of human development. Perhaps it was the beginning of what may turn out to be the end of our civilization. Which it will be depends on the decisions to be taken by leaders who are, everybody hopes, wiser than they often sound.

23
Leo

The sign of Leo, the Lion, begins now and lasts until August 23.

BIG ANIMALS

July is a fine time to visit the zoo. Most of the animals are in their best condition. Why is it that the elephants always attract such a large crowd of watchers? Is it their huge size? Their bulk is certainly one reason, and perhaps the main reason. Look at the interest people have in reading about the monsters that lived in the age of dinosaurs. Of course there is something impressive about animals that would have stood higher than a three-story building. The biggest of the dinosaurs grew to a length of nearly ninety feet, and must have weighed pretty close to fifty tons. And yet the largest animal that ever lived is living right now, and doesn't attract much interest, though he would make a dinosaur look like a lightweight. It is the blue whale. Blue whales have been harpooned that ran over a hundred feet in length, and weighed over a hundred tons.

24
BIRTHDAY OF
Simon Bolivar 1783

The Liberator was born in Caracas, Venezuela, of a noble and rich family. He was educated in Europe, and was in France during the Revolution. He also visited the United States, and was impressed by what he saw of democracy. He determined to free his country from Spanish rule. As the leader of the South American struggle for independence, he fought for years against the Spaniards. The area he helped liberate, now includes the countries of Peru, Bolivia, Venezuela, Colombia and Ecuador. Bolivar was a man of noble character. He fought for others, and not for his own benefit. Although for a time he controlled the finances of three countries—Colombia, Peru and Bolivia—he never took a cent for himself. He spent most of his own large fortune in the revolutionary cause. There is a statue of Bolivar in Central Park in New York.

Alexandre Dumas

the French novelist, was also born on July 24, but in the year 1802. He was a liberal, like Bolivar, and supported the French republic, although himself the son of one of Napoleon's generals. He joined Garibaldi's attempt to free Italy from Austria. He wrote many stories that make exciting reading. The best of them are 'The Three Musketeers' and 'The Count of Monte Cristo.'

JEREMY CRABAPPLE says:

Quick to succeed, fails just as quick:
Goes up like a rocket, comes down like the stick.

AUGUST

August is a month for travel, for vacations,
for storing up enough sun and clean air and green thoughts
to last through a year of work.
The late flowers come in, and the new fruits.
Augustus, the first Roman emperor,
named the month after himself,
because he wanted his month to follow
that of Julius Caesar, whose nephew and heir he was.

1
BIRTHDAY OF
Herman Melville 1819

Melville was born in New York City. He had some schooling, but began work in his late teens before completing his education. After a few jobs that failed to interest him he signed on a ship as a cabin boy, and sailed to England. At twenty-two he went on a long whaling voyage in the Pacific. He deserted the ship in the Marquesas Islands, on account of the cruelty of the captain. There he was captured by cannibals on the island of Nukahiva. He lived with them quite happily for several months until he was rescued by the crew of an Australian ship. He joined the ship, and two years later was back in New York.

On his return he took to writing, making use of his sea experiences. His first books, 'Typee' and 'Omoo,' were based on what he had seen among the Pacific islanders. His next, 'Mardi,' was a kind of fantasy on the same theme. Then he turned back to his first voyage, and in 'Redburn' told about a cabin boy sailing to Liverpool. These books were very popular, and made Melville a well-known writer. He settled down on a farm in Massachusetts near where Hawthorne lived, and he and Hawthorne became close friends.

The publication of his greatest book, 'Moby Dick,' changed his situation. The readers were disappointed. They expected a romantic story about some strange foreign place, like his earlier novels. They could not see the point of 'Moby Dick' at all. Melville did not regain his popularity, and published less and less as time went on. 'The Piazza Tales,' which has some wonderful short stories in it, fell flat with the public. Melville became a customs inspector in New York, retired at sixty-five and died a few years later, almost completely forgotten. Thirty years later his books were republished, and everybody saw that he was a great American writer. 'Moby Dick' is his masterpiece.

Richard Henry Dana, Jr.

another man who wrote an important book on the sea, was born on the same day as Melville, but four years earlier, in 1815. Richard Henry Dana, Jr. was a student at Harvard. Having trouble with his eyesight, he took ship as a seaman in an attempt to improve his eyes. On his return he wrote 'Two Years Before the Mast,' the story of his voyage, which gave a realistic account of the hard life of ordinary seamen. The book was widely read both in the United States and Europe, and has come to be considered a classic of the sea.

AUGUST

4
Percy Bysshe Shelley ₁₇₉₂

Although Shelley died in a sea accident at the early age of thirty, he left a large volume of poems behind him, and is one of the best poets of his time. This is how he makes the cloud speak in a poem:

I bring fresh showers for the thirsting flowers,
 From the seas and the streams;
I bear light shade for the leaves when laid
 In their noonday dreams.
From my wings are shaken the dews that waken
 The sweet buds everyone,
When rocked to rest on their mother's breast,
 As she dances about the sun.
I wield the flail of the lashing hail,
 And whiten the green plains under;
And then again I dissolve it in rain,
 And laugh as I pass in thunder.

AUGUST

THE FOUR MINUTE MILE

Would a man ever be able to run a mile in four minutes? Many people said it was impossible until Roger Bannister in 1954 ran a mile in three minutes and 59.4 seconds. Once they knew it could be done, it didn't take long for other runners to do better. Four years later, on August 6, 1958, in Dublin, Ireland, Albert Thomas ran the mile four-fifths of a second faster than Bannister, and finished a sad fifth in the race. The winner, Herb Elliott, was timed at three minutes and 54.5 seconds, which is still the world's record.

All in all, through 1959, twenty-two runners have run the mile in under four minutes, and it has been done 51 times. Only one American, Don Bowden, who made it in 1957, is in the select circle of four-minute milers.

6
BIRTHDAY OF
Alfred Lord Tennyson 1809

Tennyson was born only a few years after Shelley, but lived on almost to the end of the century. His poems are among the most musical in the English language, and all have a note of sadness. Here is his picture of the eagle:

He clasps the crag with crooked hands;
Close to the sun in lonely lands,
Ringed with the azure world, he stands.

The wrinkled sea beneath him crawls;
He watches from his mountain walls,
And like a thunderbolt he falls.

15
BIRTHDAY OF
Sir Walter Scott 1771

Scott made his reputation with his long narrative poems, 'The Lay of the Last Minstrel,' 'Marmion,' and 'The Lady of the Lake.' The stories were so interesting and the verse so lively that they became the most popular poems of their time. Scott then turned to the novel, and became the first historical novelist to have a great success. His novels found readers all over the world, and are still worth reading. 'Ivanhoe,' which children are required to read in school, is one of the poorest. Among the good ones are 'Rob Roy,' the story of a Scottish Robin Hood, 'Guy Mannering,' 'The Fortunes of Nigel,' and 'The Heart of Midlothian.'

17
BIRTHDAY OF
David Crockett 1786

The famous frontiersman, Davy Crockett, spent his early life in the backwoods of Tennessee, where he became widely known for his skill as a hunter and trapper. He fought in the Creek War under Andrew Jackson. He served two terms as a Congressman when Jackson was President. Having been defeated for reelection because he was an opponent of Jackson's policies, he joined the Texan fight for independence. He was killed in the defense of the Alamo in 1836.

AUGUST

23
Virgo

The sign of Virgo, the Virgin, begins on this date and continues until September 22.

27
BIRTHDAY OF
Confucius 551 B.C.

Confucius is the great wise man of China. He lived in a time of turmoil when China was divided into many separate states that fought with each other. He wanted to bring all China together under one just government so that its people could have a peaceful and happy life. He thought that, if one ruler were just, his subjects would respect him, and the state would become orderly and prosperous. And starting from that center, justice and order would spread out over all of China. While he never found a ruler who would put his ideas into practice, he succeeded in convincing many followers who studied under him and passed his ideas on to later generations.

Other wise men have shared some of Confucius's ideas. The remarkable thing about his thinking is the importance he assigns to language, music and poetry. He insisted there could be no justice unless words had a clear and definite meaning, and language was properly used. The main purpose of education, he said, was to make men fair and kind, and to free them from evil passions. This could be done by the proper study of poetry and music.

AUGUST

28
BIRTHDAY OF
Goethe 1749
and Tolstoi 1828

Wolfgang Goethe, the greatest of German writers, and Leo Tolstoi, the greatest of Russian writers, were born on the same day, but many years apart. Goethe was an all-around man who was interested in everything and did well at everything he tackled. He is the best of German poets, but to appreciate his poems you have to read them in the original German. He wrote good novels which can be enjoyed in English translation. One of them, 'Wilhelm Meister's Apprenticeship,' tells in fictional form about Goethe's own youth. He was a scientist, and did original work in botany and optics. He was minister of state to the Duke of Weimar, and director of the theater at Weimar. His most famous work is his poetic play, 'Faust,' which he spent over thirty years in writing. 'Faust' has been given on the stage many times, both in its original form and in many adaptations, as opera and as a musical play.

Tolstoi

was a man of very different character from Goethe. He was a reformer with a religious point of view who disliked the way of life of his time, and the modern emphasis on science and progress. He wanted a return to a simpler life. He wanted to get away from the useless life of the upper class to which he belonged and get closer to the common people who understood the real meaning of life, he thought. He had tremendous influence in his time, and many people followed his ideas.

One reason for the impression he made, and the main reason he is still read, is that he is a wonderful writer and one of the best story-tellers in the world. His masterpiece is "War and Peace," the best of all historical novels. Especially interesting to young masterpiece is 'War and Peace,' people are 'Childhood,' 'Boyhood' and 'Youth,' which are fictional accounts of his own early life.

AUGUST

BIRDLIKE SONGS

Sometimes in the country you hear sounds you may think are made by birds, but you would be surprised if you saw the 'bird.' Late at night you may hear what sounds like the hooting of screech owls. If it comes from the ground, a racoon is probably responsible. And sometimes when you're walking around the fields at night, you will hear a high thin trilling song, something like the song of the canary. Don't look around for runaway canaries. It's just mouse music.

The Chinese made paper over two thousand years ago. They passed on the secret to the Arabs who introduced the art into Spain in the twelfth century. Still, paper was made a long time before that. Anybody who has ever looked into a wasp or hornet's nest knows who the first papermakers were. The first man who made paper might well have got the idea from these pestiferous insects.

SEAWEED

Few things in the world are pleasanter than to wander along a sandy beach on a good day in August, looking at what the tide has cast up and stopping now and then for a dip in the surf to cool off. Among the many strange objects scattered on the sand some of the most interesting are the sea plants. The plants of the ocean live in a narrow belt from the high tide mark to about a hundred feet below the low tide mark. Few plants are able to live deeper than that, because the light becomes too faint to support vegetable life. The plants of the ocean need no stems; the water buoys them up. They need no roots; the water is rich in the minerals they use for food. They have no leaves to process their food; the whole plant acts as a leaf. And instead of having flowers or seeds like most land plants, they form spores like ferns and mosses.

We call them seaweeds or sea-mosses; their scientific name is algae. They all have the green substance in them that leaves have, that helps them process their food, but in some of them the green is covered by brown, red or black. The green algae live at the top of the sea where the sunlight is brightest; you find them mostly at the high tide mark. The brown and black ones grow underneath; they like the medium light between the low tide mark and a depth of about twenty feet. They cluster on top of the rocks at the low tide mark, and make them too slippery to climb on. The algae that live deepest down are the red mossy ones; these you see after a storm has thrown them up on the beach.

Some seaweeds are useful. One kind, called 'dulse' is used for food. Out of another, a substance called 'agar-agar' is made, which is eaten in the Orient and also used for chemical purposes. The ash of seaweed, called 'kelp,' is one source of iodine. In some places farmers collect seaweed and use it as a fertilizer.

JEREMY CRABAPPLE says:

*Talks-too-much shows
How little he knows.*

SEPTEMBER

September is the first month of autumn.
The sun moves south in the sky,
and many birds begin to go south.
Crops are harvested.
Fruits are ripe or ripening.
A tree here and there shows a gleam of fall color.
The name comes from the Latin word for seven,
because September was the seventh month in the Roman calendar.

SEPTEMBER

Labor Day

The first Monday in September is a national holiday in honor of the workers whose efforts support the economy of the United States. It is celebrated by parades of the labor unions in the large cities.

*A*mericans who served in the armed forces in the Pacific brought back many odd souvenirs, but none better looking than the cat's-eye. The cat's-eye, especially when it is set in a ring or pin, seems to be a precious stone. Actually it is the trap door that closes the opening of the shell of a sea snail, one variety of the turban shell snails. It protects the snail from intruders, and may even scare off its enemies because it looks like the eye of a squid.

Harvest Festival

Ever since the beginning of agriculture in the New Stone Age, men have greeted the gathering of the crops with feasting and ceremony. The ancient Jews had their harvest festival just fifty days after the second day of Passover, because wheat ripens early in Palestine. The ancient Romans had a festival in honor of Ceres, the goddess of agriculture, in August. We still call grain products 'cereals' because they were once held to be the gifts of Ceres. Everywhere farmers celebrated both the picking of the first fruits and the completion of the harvest. In our time these customs have disappeared in many places, and survive only in remote rural districts.

3
Henry
Hudson ₁₆₀₉

On this day Hudson entered New York bay. It was his third voyage in search of a Northwest Passage to China. He sailed his little ship, the *Half-Moon*, one hundred and fifty miles up the river which still bears his name. Stopping near where the city of Albany now is, Hudson had a parley with the local Indians and looked at the water above the tide level. From what he could find out he decided, rightly, that the river did not lead to the South Seas or to China and turned back.

SEPTEMBER

14
BIRTHDAY OF
Alexander von Humboldt 1769

Nobody who knew Humboldt as a child could have guessed that he would become a great explorer and scientist. His health was poor and he did not seem to be particularly bright. The only sign of his future interests was his hobby of collecting plants, shells and insects. His father, a Prusian officer who had risen to be royal chamberlain, died when Humboldt was ten. His mother, also an aristocrat, wanted him to have a political career.

Humboldt was twenty before his true bent came to the fore. At the university his mind fixed itself on natural science. And at the same time a friendship with George Forster who had been on Captain Cook's second voyage aroused his passion for travel in far and difficult places. He determined to be a scientific explorer. His new ambition brought out the full strength of his mind. With amazing speed and thoroughness he mastered all the studies he needed for his work. He learned foreign languages, geology, astronomy, anatomy, and the use of scientific instruments. He took a government position as inspector of mines and published several scientific papers that at once showed his versatility. One was a report of the vegetation of the mines of Freiberg. Another gave the results of a long series of experiments on muscular irritability.

It was not until he was nearly thirty that his mother's death left him free to set out on his first expedition. With one companion he started a journey that was to last over five years. In South America the two men followed the course of the Orinoco River, a trip of 1,725 miles in wild country. They sailed to Cuba and spent a few months there. Returning to South America, they traveled up the Magdalena River, made the difficult crossing of the Cordilleras and reached Quito. They climbed two mountain peaks, Pichincha and Chimborazo, and on the way to Lima explored the sources of the Amazon. From Lima they sailed up the west coast to Mexico where they stayed a year. After a visit to the United States they returned to Europe.

Humboldt thought it would take him two years to write up the mass of materials and observations he had collected. It took twenty-one years and the job was not fully completed. Publication made him one of the most famous men in Europe. He used his prestige wisely; he was the first man to secure international cooperation in a great scientific project; the study of magnetic storms. He was sixty before he went on his next expedition, which was also his last. He crossed the entire width of the Russian Empire in twenty-five weeks, making some valuable geological observations despite the speed of the journey.

For years Humboldt planned a big book describing the physical structure of the world. He started writing it at seventy-six. Two years later he published the first two volumes of his master work 'Kosmos.' Humboldt lived to be almost ninety and worked almost to the end, adding two more volumes to 'Kosmos' as well as the greater part of a third which was published after his death. He made contributions to almost every branch of natural science, but his lasting fame is as the real founder of the sciences of physical geography and meteorology.

16
BIRTHDAY OF
Tintoretto 1518

Tintoretto, the name by which he is still known, was a nickname he got as a child. His father, Battista Robusti, was a dyer and so the son, Jacopo Robusti, was called Tintoretto, which means 'little dyer' in Italian. He showed his passion for painting early, doing pictures on the walls of his father's shop. His father took him to the greatest painter of Venice, Titian, to be trained as an artist. After a few days Titian sent him home, refusing to teach him. The reason is not known; the notion that Titian was jealous of the boy's talent is one rumor. It is much more likely that Titian felt that Tintoretto would not profit from his teaching, because his abilities lay in a different direction. Tintoretto never tried to find another teacher. He studied and practiced alone, drawing and modeling in wax and clay. He lived in great

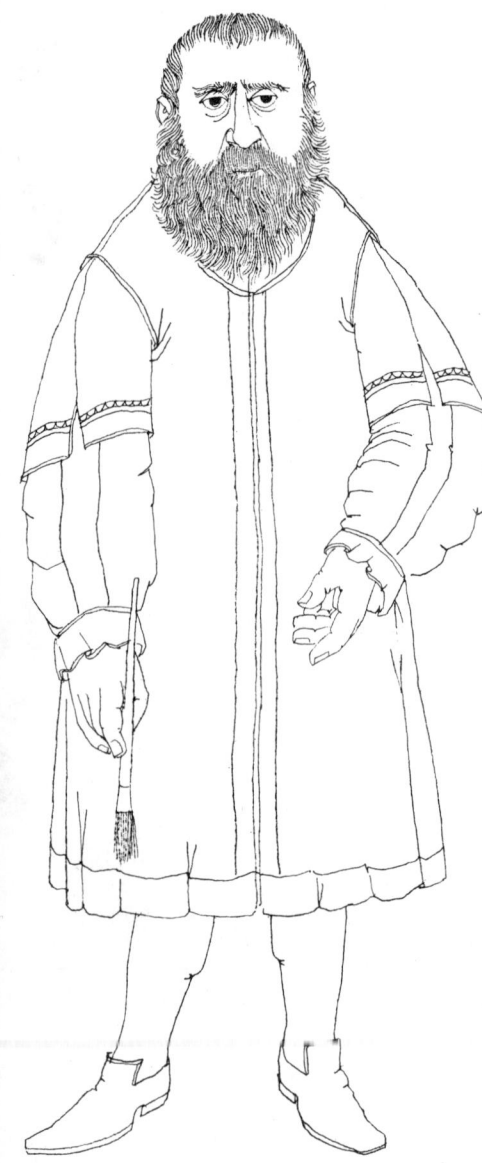

poverty, working day and night. He expressed his ambition in the sign he put up in his studio: 'The design of Michelangelo and the color of Titian.'

He got his start as a professional painter by working without pay. And even after he became famous he showed little interest in money. He painted his enormous picture *Paradise* for the city of Venice. He was asked to name his own price. He said he would take whatever the senators wished to give. When the payment was made Tintoretto returned some of the money. *Paradise* is held to be the largest picture ever painted on canvas. It is seventy-four feet wide and thirty feet high.

Tintoretto painted with such furious energy that he was called 'Il furioso.' The sheer quantity of painting he did, and the speed with which he did it, is incredible. Sebastiano del Piombo, another fine painter of his time, said that Tintoretto could paint more in two days than he himself could in two years. Tintoretto lived in a retired way, sticking to his studio most of the time even when he was not painting. Although he showed no taste for social life, he was a man of great personal charm and witty in his conversation. He was a lover of all the arts. He played the lute and other musical instruments, some of them of his own invention.

SEPTEMBER

17
Constitution Day

On this day in 1781 the United States Constitution, drafted by the Constitutional Convention in Philadelphia, was signed. On June 21, 1788 when it had been ratified by nine states, it replaced the Articles of Confederation and became the basis of our government. The Constitution tells how the states are related to each other and to the federal government, and gives the powers and duties of the executive, legislative and judicial branches of the government. The first ten amendments, called the Bill of Rights, state the basic rights of the people.

21
Autumnal Equinox

On this day the sun moves into a position in the sky so that day and night are equal in length.

23
Libra

The sun now enters the sign of Libra, the Scales, and stays in this sign of the zodiac until October 23.

23
BIRTHDAY OF
Euripides <small>480 B.C.</small>

We know the birth date of Euripides because it is said that he was born on the very day the Greeks defeated the Persians in the great sea battle of Salamis. He is the last of the three most famous dramatists of the ancient world. The first, Aeschylus, was the founder of tragedy. Seven of his plays are still known. One of them, 'The Persians' celebrates the battle of Salamis in which Aeschylus himself fought. The second great Greek dramatist was Sophocles, and we have only seven of the more than hundred plays he wrote. Euripides, the last of the three, is said to have written ninety-two plays; we have nineteen left.

All drama since their time owes something to the work of these three great masters. Their plays remain a permanent inspiration and a model of what is best in the art.

SEPTEMBER

25 Balboa discovers the Pacific 1513

The Spanish explorer, Balboa, crossed the isthmus of Panama with a band of Spaniards and Indians. He was looking for gold but instead on this day he found the Pacific Ocean: 'the South Sea,' the western route to the orient that many explorers had been searching for.

THE CLINGING BARNACLE

The most common sea animal found on any rocky seashore is the barnacle. And you will also find them attached to the bottom of boats, the supports of wharves or any other object under water that they can cling to. Barnacles are not related to clams or oysters, though they have a hard shell. They belong to the same family as crabs and shrimps. When a baby barnacle hatches from its egg, it swims around as a small sea animal with one eye, three pairs of legs and a shell. After molting a few times, it has two eyes, six pairs of legs and two shells. When it finds a rock that will do for a home, it attaches its front to the rock, makes a cement that will hold it fast, grows its permanent shell and stays put, kicking its food into its mouth with its legs. If you've ever tried to pry a barnacle loose, you know why people say of anybody that clings that he hangs on 'like a barnacle.'

JEREMY CRABAPPLE says:

*Those who always sing in a crowd
never know the sound of their own voices.*

OCTOBER

October is the month of falling leaves.
The earth comes into its full autumn colors,
red and yellow and brown.
The sky seems to turn a deeper blue,
as the winds blow and the clouds race.
We get its name from the ancient Romans.
It was the eighth month in the old Roman calendar,
and October comes from a Latin word meaning eight.

OCTOBER

2

BIRTHDAY OF

Gandhi 1869

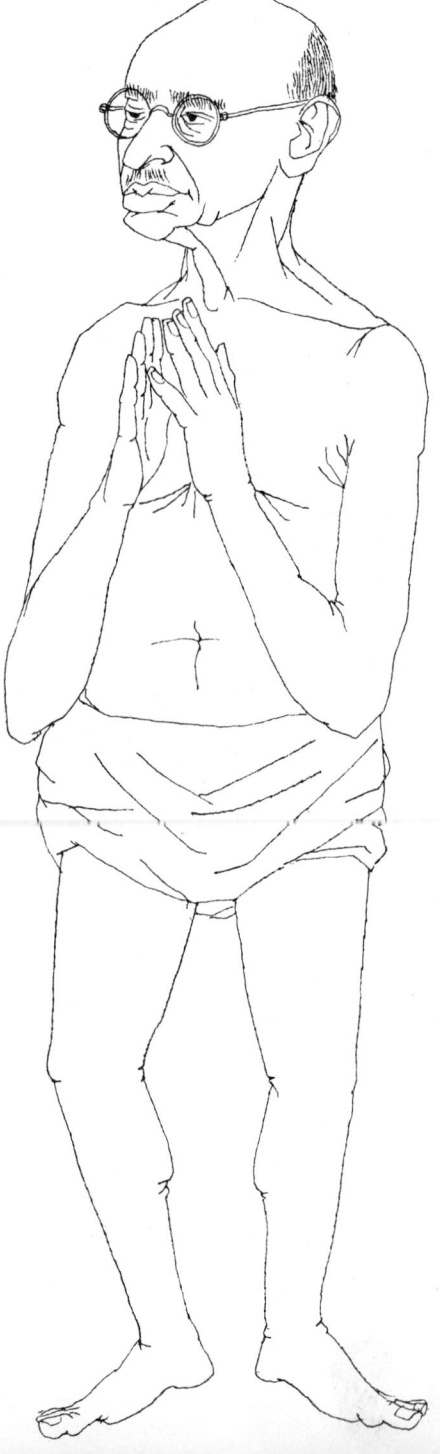

Mohandas Karamchand Gandhi was not the kind of man you would expect to find as the leader of a struggle for independence. He was opposed to any form of violence. He was an intensely religious man, and led the life of an ascetic. The Indian people looked on Gandhi as a saint and called him *Mahatma* which means 'great soul.' He urged his followers to strike at the roots of British rule by boycotting anything British, the manufactures as well as the government offices. They were to learn to use the spinning wheel and to make their own cloth, rather than help British commerce by buying British cloth. At the same time they were not to do anything violent and to submit peacefully to arrest and imprisonment. And when India finally gained its independence, Gandhi preferred to let Pakistan go its own way and form its own state rather than to have a civil war.

Some European and American thinkers have been influenced by Gandhi's ideas, and feel that a peaceful way of settling political differences is better than violence. But even those who think differently recognize that Mahatma Gandhi was a great man, and his ideas noble, though sometimes hard to put into practice.

OCTOBER

4
Feast of St. Francis

This feast is celebrated in memory of St. Francis of Assisi who was born on this day in the year 1181 or 1182. He was the son of a merchant, and spent his youth in sport and amusement. At twenty he fought for his native city Assisi in a battle with the neighboring city of Perugia. The men of Assisi lost, and Francis was captured and spent a year in prison. On his release he returned to Assisi and to his old merry life. Shortly afterwards he fell ill and during his illness began to be uneasy about his way of life. One day he gave a banquet for his friends. They went into the streets carrying torches and singing, with Francis crowned with garlands as their leader. After a while they lost him and went looking for him. They found him in a trance, a completely changed man. From that time forth he devoted himself to prayer and service to the poor. He went on a pilgrimage to Rome. In front of St. Peter's, he exchanged clothes with a beggar and spent the rest of the day begging. In time, disciples gathered about him and he formed the Franciscan Order of monks, and later of nuns, who chose a life of poverty and prayer, preaching and serving the poor.

Among the saints it is hard to find another who tried so wholeheartedly to lead the life of Christ. St. Francis did not merely accept poverty, he actually loved it. Everything he did he did with joy, spending much of his time singing. He looked on everything in the world as his sisters and brothers. In his poem 'Praise of the Creatures,' he asks 'brother Sun,' 'sister Moon,' 'brother Wind' and 'sister Water' to praise God.

OCTOBER

9

BIRTHDAY OF

Cervantes

1547

Miguel de Cervantes Saavedra was the greatest of Spain's novelists and a fine poet and playwright. One book of his, 'Don Quixote,' belongs to all of mankind. It is a strange story, very spirited and funny on the surface, with a deep note of pity and sadness underneath. The mad knight, Don Quixote, and his peasant squire, Sancho Panza, in their absurd adventures show us a picture of the variety and muddle of human life. It is one of the great books of the world. Children can read it just for amusement, and older people read it for its profound understanding of the nature of man.

Cervantes saw a good deal of life before he wrote the book. At twenty-four he was a soldier in the armada of Don John of Austria. When the battle of Lepanto began he was lying below, ill with fever. He insisted on joining in the battle, fought bravely and got three wounds, two in the chest and one that permanently crippled his right hand. After four more years in the army he was given leave to return home. On the way his ship was attacked by Barbary pirates, and Cervantes was captured and sold into slavery in Algiers. Cervantes made several attempts to escape. He might have been executed if the viceroy of Algiers had not been impressed by his courage. After five years the large ransom demanded for him was paid and Cervantes returned to Spain. It was then, in middle life, that he began writing.

OCTOBER

FALL FLOWERS

At the time when the grass is beginning to lose its fresh green and the leaves are beginning to turn yellow and red and brown, the autumn flowers bring two bright colors: the purple of asters and the gold of goldenrod. There are more asters and goldenrod than any other autumn flowers. Over two hundred kinds of asters, ranging in color from deep purple to almost pure white, crowd the dry fields and open woods. And over a hundred kinds of goldenrod spread over the fields and hillsides. There are other flowers that add their touch of color too. The common milkweed, which grows almost anywhere but especially likes waste places, is purple. In swamps and wet ground its cousin, the swamp milkweed has a red flower. Another cousin, the butterfly weed, likes dry places and sports an orange flower. Two common flowers which like sunny places, yarrow and Queen Anne's lace, are white.

12
Columbus Day

We celebrate the discovery of the New World on this day; the day in 1492 when Columbus landed at San Salvador with his three ships, the *Santa Maria*, the *Pinta* and the *Nina*.

OCTOBER

19
BIRTHDAY OF
John Adams *1735*

John Adams is one of the greatest of the founding fathers of the United States. In intellectual ability he is close to Franklin and Jefferson; in courage and sense of honor he is close to Washington. He was one of the earliest advocates of American Independence. He helped write the Declaration of Independence. He concluded the treaty of peace with England and served as Minister to England. He was the first Vice-President of the United States, and its second President.

His descendants have included eminent men in every generation. The most important of them are: his son, John Quincy Adams who was sixth President of the United States; his grandson, Charles Francis Adams who was Minister to Great Britain; and his great-grandson, Henry Adams who was a famous historian.

OCTOBER

23
Scorpio

The sun now enters the sign of Scorpio, the Scorpion, and moves in this sign of the zodiac until November 22.

27
BIRTHDAY OF
Paganini ₁₇₈₂

Nicolo Paganini was probably the greatest violinist of all time. He began to study the instrument when he was very young. His father, who was a good amateur player, was his first teacher. He first played in public when he was nine. From the beginning he was a remarkable performer, and he kept improving rapidly.

He began touring through Europe in his early twenties, and made a sensation wherever he played. Much of what he played was of his own composition, and some of the pieces were so difficult that very few violinists have been able to play them properly since Paganini's time. Besides astonishing audiences with his tremendous feats of virtuosity he moved them to tears with his affecting performance of emotional passages. His looks had an effect too: he was tall, abnormally thin, with an impressive face and long black hair. All sorts of fanciful stories were told about him; one was that he had made a pact with the devil. The truth is much simpler. He was a man of extraordinary musical talent, both as performer and composer, and he practiced endless hours to perfect his amazing skill.

29
BIRTHDAY OF
John Keats 1795

Keats was the son of a livery-stable keeper. He was studying to be a doctor when he met Leigh Hunt, an older poet, and decided to give up medicine and devote himself to poetry. He had only a short time to do his work. He was suffering from tuberculosis, and at that time they did not know how to treat the disease. In the space of a few years he wrote many fine poems. His poetry kept growing better so rapidly that many critics feel he would have been one of the greatest of English poets if he had lived longer. He died in Rome in his twenty-sixth year and is buried in the English Cemetery there, not far from Shelley.

31
Halloween

Before Christianity came into Britain the people had another religion. The old religion was the Druid religion, and it died out so completely after the coming of Christianity that little is now known of its actual beliefs and ceremonies. One of the few remaining Druid customs was the lighting of bonfires on Halloween, which was the night before the Druid autumn festival. It was believed that ghosts and witches went around during this night.

JEREMY CRABAPPLE says:

> *What other time in times gone by*
> *Can match our time in worth,*
> *That sports its sputniks in the sky*
> *And beatniks on the earth?*

NOVEMBER

*November takes us close to the edge of winter,
but it often has days
that bring back a touch of summer.
And there are days of high wind, true autumn days,
when the crisp air makes us tingle as we breathe.
The name of November
comes from the Latin word for nine because it was
the ninth month in old Roman calendar.*

NOVEMBER

2
BIRTHDAY OF
Daniel Boone *1734*

Daniel Boone was a famous hunter, trapper, woodsman and Indian fighter, who helped found settlements as Americans moved west, pushing back the Indians and taking over new land.

5
Guy Fawkes Day

Guy Fawkes was one of a group of conspirators who dug a tunnel under the British House of Lords with the idea of blowing it up while it was in session. He was caught on this night in 1605 and executed a few days later. The whole affair is known in British history as the 'Gunpowder Plot.' British schoolboys still celebrate the night by building bonfires and burning effigies of Guy Fawkes.

Indian Summer

It is about this time of the year that we get a stretch of warm dry weather with little wind and usually a bit of haze in the air. In the United States we call it 'Indian Summer.' In England, France and Italy they call it 'St. Martin's Summer.'

13
BIRTHDAY OF
Stevenson 1850

Robert Louis Stevenson was a fine poet and novelist who wrote some of his best things for children. His book, 'A Child's Garden of Verses,' has in it many of the most delightful simple poems in the English language. Everybody has to read 'Treasure Island' in school, and it's no hardship. And many children go on to find 'Kidnapped' and 'David Balfour' and 'The Black Arrow.'

Stevenson spent the latter part of his life struggling against tuberculosis. He traveled among the Pacific islands, looking for a climate that would suit his frail health. He settled in Samoa where he is buried under the epitaph he wrote for himself:

Here he lies where he longed to be;
Home is the sailor, home from the sea,
And the hunter home from the hill.

Thanksgiving

Americans set aside the last Thursday in November to give thanks to God, following a tradition which began with the Pilgrim Fathers. The Pilgrims had landed on December 21, 1620. They went through a hard winter. It was not until the harvest was in in 1621 that they felt secure. They decided to set aside a day of thanksgiving. Indian friends brought in some wild turkeys which they had shot and these provided the main course of the feast. And so to this day turkey is the main dish of the thanksgiving dinner.

ZOOS

The notion of keeping wild animals in captivity is very old. We can see from Egyptian tomb inscriptions that this was done as early as four thousand years ago. There is the record of a zoo in China about three thousand years ago. And it is said that the philosopher Aristotle had a zoo, and his pupil Alexander the Great used to send him animals from the places he conquered.

But it is only in modern times that really big zoos with enormous collections of animals have been built up. The biggest in the world today is the collection of the Zoological Society of London which has over three thousand different kinds of animals. The biggest zoo in the United States is the Bronx Zoo with about a thousand different kinds of animals.

22
Sagittarius

On this day the sun enters the sign of Sagittarius, the Archer, and stays in this area of the zodiac until December 22.

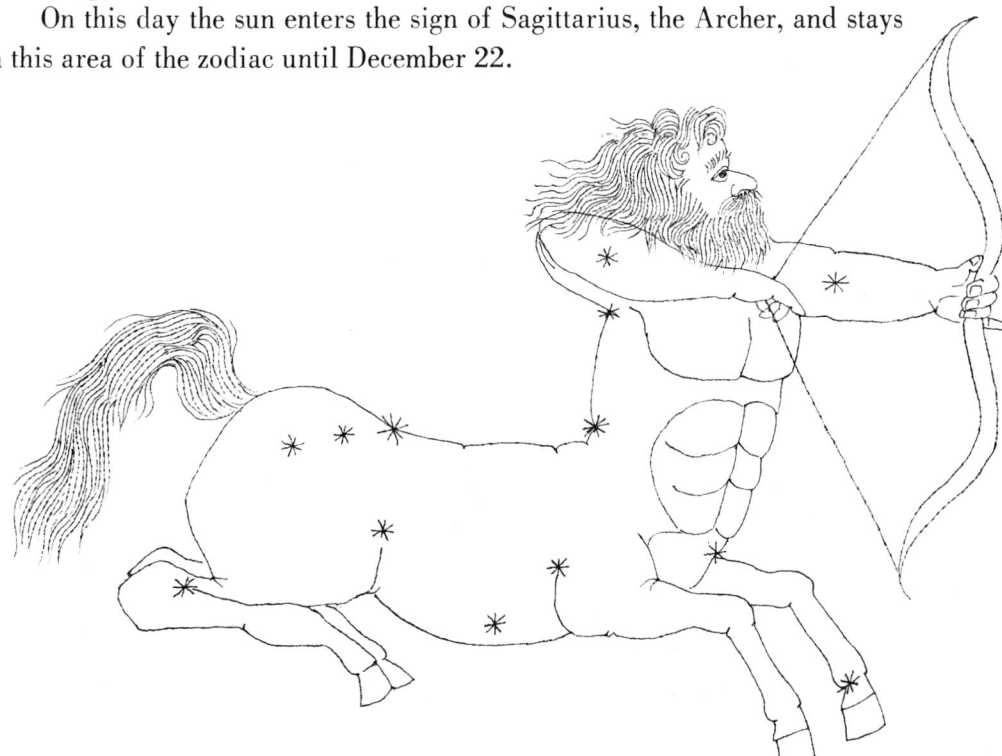

NOVEMBER

29
BIRTHDAY OF
Louisa May Alcott 1832

Louisa May Alcott, a New England writer, wrote many books for children. The best ones are about the March family and are based on her own childhood. The first of these, 'Little Women,' is a book which many girls like, and even some boys.

30
BIRTHDAY OF
Mark Twain 1835

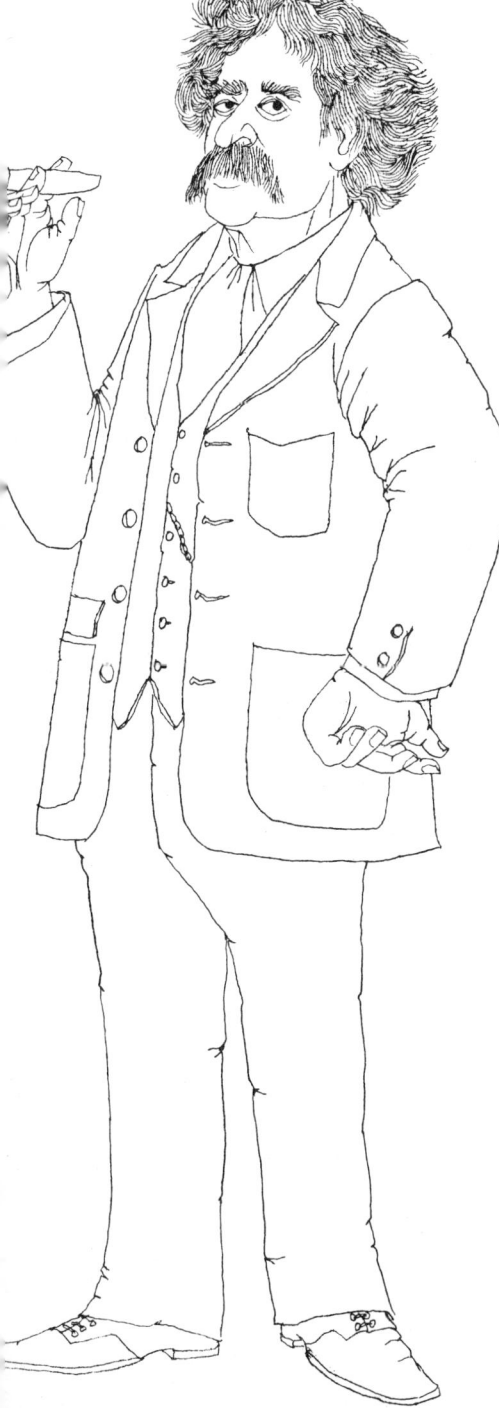

His real name was Samuel Langhorne Clemens. He was born in Missouri, the son of a country storekeeper. His father died when he was twelve, and from that time on he was on his own. He learned how to set type, and worked as a printer until he was nineteen. Then he succeeded in achieving his childhood ambition, and became a pilot on the Mississippi River. The Civil War put an end to the piloting. He headed west, and worked in the mines in Nevada. In Nevada he began to write for the newspapers, using 'Mark Twain' as a pen name. It was a call used by the man who took soundings of the depth of the water to guide the pilot.

For the rest of his life Mark Twain divided his time between writing and lecturing.

His first book, 'The Innocents Abroad,' made him widely popular, and he began to appear on the lecture platform where his easy-going way of talking and his many funny stories were much liked. His best books are the books based on his childhood, 'The Adventures of Tom Sawyer' and 'Huckleberry Finn.' But there are many others worth reading, among them 'Pudd'nhead Wilson' and 'A Connecticut Yankee in King Arthur's Court.' And for those who have a special liking for his humor there are his travel books, his essays and his book of short stories.

NOVEMBER

THE MIGRATION OF BIRDS

•Some birds are very hardy, and spend the winter in the north. The chickadee, for instance, stays in the same place all the year round. And nuthatches and blue jays can manage to get through the winter without freezing or starving. This is easier around cities where people put out food or wherever there are lots of trees or bushes with seeds and berries on them. Some birds that are with us in the winter, such as the junco and the snow bunting, actually like the cold, and spend their summers far north.

Most birds, however, go south in the winter. They get ready for their trip by putting on extra fat and by molting, which is changing their bright summer coat for a duller winter one. That's why the tanagers, the buntings and the warblers seem to disappear towards the end of the summer. They haven't started south yet. They've begun to molt, losing their brightly colored feathers and replacing them with dull grayish ones.

So many thousands of birds migrate that you may wonder why we don't see great flocks passing over in the fall. The reason is that most birds in migrating travel at night and rest by day. They have hundreds of miles to go, and they take it easy on the way. The most remarkable thing about bird migration is that many birds move thousands of miles in their yearly migration, and yet find their way back to their own home spots without any trouble.

How do they do it? Is it instinct? Do they follow landmarks, like rivers or mountains? Do they have a built-in sense of direction? We don't really know the whole answer. Perhaps all those things play their part.

Have you noticed how beautiful trees look in winter with their bony branches stiff against the sky? They show more of their shape than when they are covered with leaves.

The highest waterfall in the world is Angel Falls in Venezuela. The water drops straight downward for a distance of nearly a mile.

The chrysanthemum has been a favorite flower in China for more than 1,500 years. It is an emblem of autumn, and often appears in Chinese painting and poetry. It even appears in Chinese food. There is a soup of meat and vegetables in which chrysanthemum petals are sprinkled.

EARLY SHIPS

The earliest record we have of ships is Egyptian, and goes back over five thousand years. They used a square-rigged sail, and oars when there was no wind. After the Egyptians the people who did the most to develop ships and the art of navigation were the Phoenicians. A Phoenician ship under Hanno the Carthaginian was the first to sail around the Cape of Good Hope, rounding the coast of Africa. All the early ships stuck pretty close to shore, relying mostly on sighting landmarks for their navigation. It was not until the age of discovery in the Fifteenth Century that European ships set out on long voyages out of sight of land. Long before that the Polynesians had begun the long voyages in their large double ships with which they colonized the Pacific islands. These voyages must have been made at least a thousand years ago, and perhaps more, at a time when Europeans were still keeping pretty close to land unless blown out to sea by bad weather.

JEREMY CRABAPPLE says:

The best rider sometimes takes a fall.

DECEMBER

December is the first month of winter.
The earth is bare and the trees leafless.
We turn to indoor occupations and pleasures more and more.
But a good snow will take us out again for sliding,
snowballing, building snow forts and snowmen, and skiing.
And in the absence of snow we can still ice-skate.
The name of the month comes from the Latin word for ten, because
December was the tenth month in the old Roman calendar.

6
Feast of St. Nicholas

St. Nicholas is our Santa Claus. In Holland, Belgium and parts of Germany it is on the eve of this feast that Christmas presents are given. The Dutch brought the custom here when they founded New York. In the course of time the custom of giving presents shifted from the eve of St. Nicholas to Christmas, and St. Nicholas moved along too, with his name changing from the Dutch 'San Nicolaas' to Santa Claus.

DECEMBER

8
BIRTHDAY OF
Joel Chandler Harris 1848

Joel Chandler Harris wrote the Uncle Remus stories. He found his inspiration in Negro folklore and caught its delightful mixture of humor, poetry and philosophy. His Uncle Remus is a wonderful character, real and full of simple charm.

DIAMONDS

The hardest substance known is the diamond, which is 90 times harder than corundum, the next hardest stone. The diamond has been regarded as a precious stone since ancient times, because it is the most brilliant and the most lasting of stones. And yet its full brilliance was not known until the middle of the eighteenth century when it was first properly cut in facets, so as to bring out all the glitter. Its hardness makes the diamond so useful in industry that it is frequently used for drilling, grinding and polishing in spite of its high price. The largest white diamond ever found was the Cullinan, found in South Africa in 1905, which weighed over a pound and a quarter and came to 3106 carats. One piece of it, called the Star of Africa, and set in the British Royal Sceptre, is the largest cut diamond in the world, having 74 facets and 330 carats.

For all it value the diamond is no more than a cousin to coal, being pure carbon chemically.

Judo, sometimes called jiujitsu, is the Japanese system of defense without the use of weapons. A small man who is skilled in judo can easily beat a larger and stronger man who is not. The skill is based on knowledge of the structure of the body. The opponent's attack is shifted by slight quick twists and grips so as to make his own force hurt himself.

DECEMBER

16
Boston Tea Party

The Boston Tea Party was the liveliest one of the anti-British demonstrations that led up to the American Revolution. In 1773 Parliament gave the East India Company the only right to sell tea in the colonies. The colonists were annoyed by this, not only because they could buy their tea more cheaply from other sources, but because it was a disguised way of taxing them, and they were opposed to taxation without representation. A band of Boston men dressed up as Indians, boarded a ship in Boston harbor, and dumped overboard 342 chests of tea. Parliament replied by passing still more oppressive measures, which led to the Revolutionary War.

DECEMBER

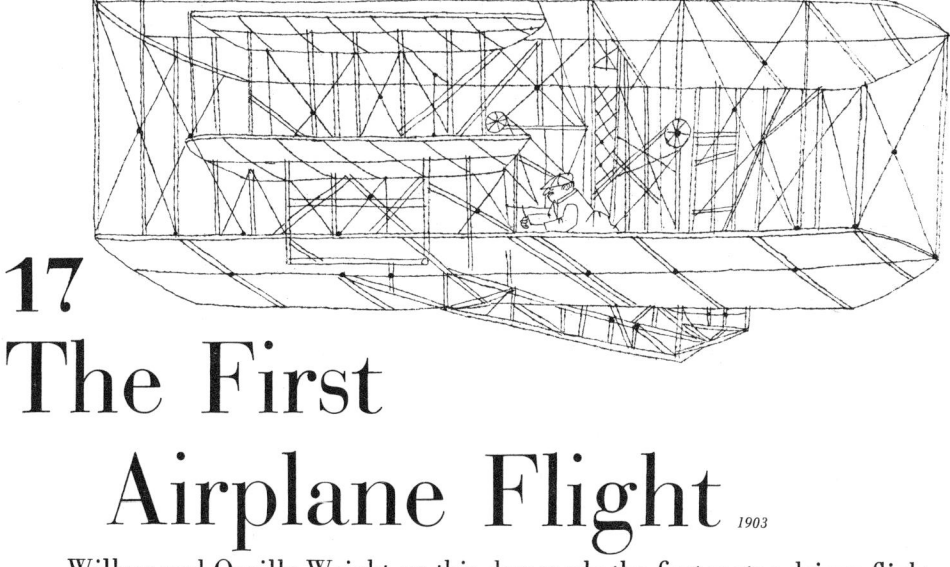

17
The First Airplane Flight ₁₉₀₃

Wilbur and Orville Wright on this day made the first motor-driven flight of a heavier-than-air ship at Kitty Hawk, North Carolina. Orville flew the ship which had been designed and built by both the brothers. It went up about eight to twelve feet, hit a speed of just over thirty miles an hour, and landed after traveling 850 feet.

21
Winter Solstice

Winter officially begins, and the sun enters the sign of Capricorn, the Goat, and stays in this sign of the zodiac until January 20.

DECEMBER

25
Christmas

Christians celebrate the birth of Christ with the good cheer known to all, and sing such carols as:

>	*God rest you merry, gentlemen*
>	*Let nothing you dismay,*
>	*Remember Christ our Savior*
>	*Was born on Christmas Day,*
>	*To save poor souls from Satan's power*
>	*Which had long time gone astray,*
>	*And it's tidings of comfort and joy, comfort and joy*
>	*And it's tidings of comfort and joy.*

SEVEN WONDERS OF THE WORLD

In ancient times there were seven extraordinary things that were called 'the seven wonders of the world.' These were the Egyptian pyramids, the hanging gardens of Babylon, the temple of Diana at Ephesus, the statue of Zeus by Phidias at Olympia, the Mausoleum at Halicarnassus, the Colossus of Rhodes, and the Pharos of Alexandria.

Four of them are gone without leaving a trace behind them. The Mausoleum and the Temple of Diana at Ephesus have left a few fragments. Only the pyramids of Egypt still stand.

THE LONGEST RIVER

The longest river in the world is the Nile, which is 4,145 miles from its source to the sea. The Amazon River is next with 3,900 miles. The Mississippi is the longest river in the United States, flowing 3,892 miles.

DECEMBER

27
BIRTHDAY OF
Louis Pasteur 1822

Louis Pasteur, the founder of modern bacteriology, was a great French chemist. He was a nervous and excitable boy, handicapped by poor health, and showed no special ability in school. But he worked hard and never gave up. Step by step he moved toward his goal: scientific research. He was only a laboratory assistant when he made his first discovery, solving a problem which had baffled all the famous physicists and chemists of the day. He was appointed a professor of chemistry, and given greater facilities for research. He went on to make one important discovery after another, all of them valuable to mankind. The basic thing he proved is that germs cause infection and fermentation. As a result we have the process that keeps milk from going sour and from carrying disease. Every time we ask for a bottle of pasteurized milk, we remember his name. In middle age Pasteur suffered a stroke, and lost the use of half his brain. With the half that was left he made some of his most impressive discoveries.

He kept working to the very end of his life. His last words to the students standing at his bedside were: 'You must work.'

29
BIRTHDAY OF
Pablo Casals 1876

    Casals, the great Spanish cellist, is famous both as a musician and a man. To hear him play and conduct, many people journey to the annual festival in Puerto Rico where he now lives as a refugee from Franco's Spain. There are good records of his playing that you can listen to.

DECEMBER

30
BIRTHDAY OF
Rudyard Kipling 1865

Kipling is a great writer who wrote most of his best things for children. He was born and brought up in India. His early childhood memories provide the most vivid details in his writing. For little children he wrote 'Just So Stories,' lively and funny stories almost like folk tales. His 'Jungle Books' tell the adventures of a boy, Mowgli, who was brought up by wolves; how he got on with all the animals of the jungle and how he finally returned to the world of man. It is a wonderful book, and enough in itself to make Kipling loved by all readers. But in 'Kim' he wrote something even better. 'Kim' is an adventure novel which takes all India as its background. The boy Kim in his wanderings meets all sorts of people and sees all sides of India.

All of Kipling is worth reading. In 'Puck of Pook's Hill' and 'Rewards and Fairies' he brings to life scenes of English history in a connected set of exciting stories. 'Captains Courageous,' his one American novel for boys, is a good story of New England fishermen. 'Stalky and Co.' is a set of stories about boys in an English school. Some of you, when you have read all that Kipling has written for children, will want to go on and read his other books as well. A good one to start with is 'Soldiers Three,' his book of stories about British soldiers in India.

DECEMBER

A SONG FOR DECEMBER

And now is come the end of the year
So blow, December, blow!
Cover the earth with a carpet of snow.
You may blow as cold and as hard as you please,
You may blow till our toes and the puddles freeze,
And the snow and our heads are spinning,
As long as you bring us our Christmas cheer
And an end that is just a beginning,
The eve of a good New Year.

WINTER SLEEP

It is hard to say whether, strictly speaking, bears hibernate. They retire to their dens for the winter and sleep, true enough. But some animals that hibernate do much more than that, or perhaps it would be better to say, much less than that. A woodchuck, for example, crawls down into its burrow and goes to sleep. As its sleep grows deeper it keeps losing body heat. At the deepest point its temperature may go down as much as fifty degrees. It breathes less and less often until it is taking only about ten breaths an hour. Its blood circulates slowly and unevenly. It comes as close to death as is possible without dying. That is full hibernation. Many animals hibernate, among them bats, chipmunks, hedgehogs, some reptiles, some insects, and even some birds. If you want to say the bear hibernates, you can, but it is only the mildest sort of hibernation, little more than a long and deep sleep.

COLD RECORD

The lowest temperature ever recorded is 108° below zero at Oimekron, Siberia, in 1938. It probably gets even colder than that on the Central Greenland Ice-cap, but so far nobody has particularly wanted to stay there all winter to take the temperature.

DECEMBER

31
New Year's Eve

The celebration of the coming of the new year, with the traditional noise- and merry-making at midnight.

JEREMY CRABAPPLE says:

The longest night
Ends in light.

PEOPLE AND DATES

ADAMS John	October 19
ALCOTT Louisa May	November 29
ANDERSEN Hans Christian	April 2
BALBOA Vasco Nunez	September 25
BAYARD Pierre Terrail de	April 30
BOLIVAR Simon	July 24
BOONE Daniel	November 2
BUDDHA	April 8
BURNS Robert	January 25
CARROLL Lewis	January 21
CARUSO Enrico	February 25
CASALS Pablo	December 29
CERVANTES SAAVEDRA Miguel de	October 9
CONFUCIUS	August 27
CROCKETT Davy	August 17
DANA Richard Henry, Jr.	August 1
DICKENS Charles	February 7
DUMAS Alexander	July 24
EDISON Thomas Alva	February 11
EINSTEIN Albert	March 14
EURIPIDES	September 23

PEOPLE AND DATES *(continued)*

FAWKES Guy	November 5
FRANCIS Saint	October 4
FRANKLIN Benjamin	January 17
GANDHI Mohandas Karamchanda	October 2
GOETHE Wolfgang von	August 28
HANDEL George Frederick	February 23
HARDY Thomas	June 2
HARRIS Chandler Joel	December 8
HOUDINI Harry	April 6
HUDSON Henry	September 3
HUMBOLDT Alexander von	September 14
JEFFERSON Thomas	April 13
JESUS	December 25
KEATS John	October 29
KIPLING Rudyard	December 30
LA FONTAINE Jean de	July 8
LEAR Edward	May 12
LEE Robert E.	January 19
LINCOLN Abraham	February 12
LINDBERGH Charles	May 21
LORENZINI Carlo	July 7

PEOPLE AND DATES (continued)

MELBA Nellie	May 19
MELVILLE Herman	August 1
MICHELANGELO	March 6
MOHAMMED	June 7
MOZART Wolfgang Amedeus	January 27
NIJINSKY Vaslav	February 28
PAGANINI Nicolo	October 27
PASTEUR Louis	December 27
PERRAULT Charles	January 12
PYLE Howard	March 5
REMBRANDT VAN RIJN	July 15
RUBENS Peter Paul	June 29
SCOTT Walter	August 15
SHAKESPEARE William	April 23
SHELLEY Percy Bysshe	August 4
STEVENSON Robert Louis	November 13
TENNYSON Alfred	August 6
TINTORETTO	September 16
TOLSTOI Leo	August 28
TOSCANINI Arturo	June 25
TWAIN Mark	November 30

PEOPLE AND DATES (continued)

           VESPUCCI Amerigo   June 16

           WASHINGTON George   February 22
           WRIGHT Frank Lloyd   June 8
           WRIGHT Orville and Wilbur   December 17

PTEMBER 23 OC
EMBER 8 JANUA
ARCH 5 APRIL 1
UGUST 17 SEPTE
OVEMBER 29 DE
FEBRUARY 22 M
MAY 12 JUNE 16
EPTEMBER 14 OC
ECEMBER 25 JAN
MARCH 6 APRI
JULY 15 AUGUST